IMAGES
of America

LIGHTHOUSES
AND LIFE SAVING
ALONG THE CONNECTICUT
AND RHODE ISLAND COAST

NOTICE TO MARINERS.

(No. 45.)

LIGHT DISCONTINUED.

TREASURY DEPARTMENT,
OFFICE LIGHT-HOUSE BOARD,
Washington, October 5, 1859.

The 3d section of the act of Congress, approved March 3, 1859, making appropriations for "light-houses, light-boats, buoys, &c.," authorized the Secretary of the Treasury, in his discretion, on the recommendation of the Light-house Board, to discontinue, from time to time, such lights as may become useless, by reason of mutations of commerce, and changes of channels of harbors, and other causes.

The Light-house Board, at its meeting held on the 3d instant, recommended that the following light be discontinued, viz:

The light at New Haven long wharf, (Conn.) It is therefore ordered and directed that the aforesaid light be discontinued on and after the first day of November next.

By order of the Secretary of the Treasury:

R. SEMMES,
Secretary.

This notice, issued by the U.S. Light-House Board on October 5, 1859, announces the discontinuing of the light at Long Wharf in New Haven, Connecticut.

On the cover: Muscle Bed Shoals Light in Mount Hope Bay, Rhode Island, is shown *c.* 1880. (Author's collection.)

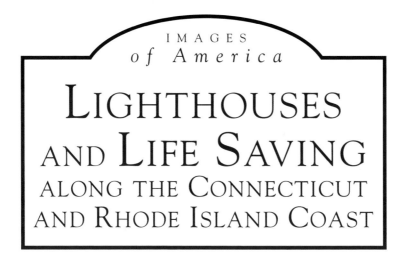

IMAGES
of America

LIGHTHOUSES
AND LIFE SAVING
ALONG THE CONNECTICUT
AND RHODE ISLAND COAST

James Claflin

ARCADIA

First published 2001
Reprinted 2004

Published by Arcadia Publishing,
Charleston SC, Chicago IL, Portsmouth NH, San Francisco CA

Printed in Great Britain

Library of Congress Catalog Card Number: 2001089669

For all general information, contact Arcadia Publishing:
Telephone 843-853-2070
Fax 843-853-0044
E-mail sales@arcadiapublishing.com
For customer service and orders:
Toll-free 1-888-313-2665

Visit us on the Internet at www.arcadiapublishing.com

This book is dedicated to the surfmen and keepers,
and to the men and women of the Coast Guard
who carry on the tradition.

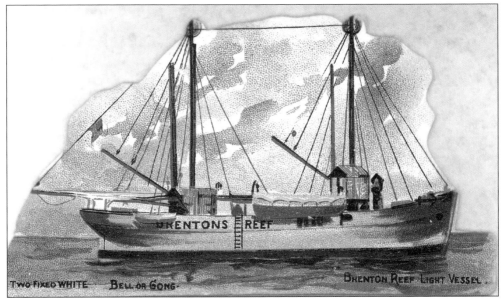

This early-1880s die-cut trade card for Honest Long Cut Tobacco shows Rhode Island's
Brenton Reef Light Vessel No. 11. (Author's collection.)

4

CONTENTS

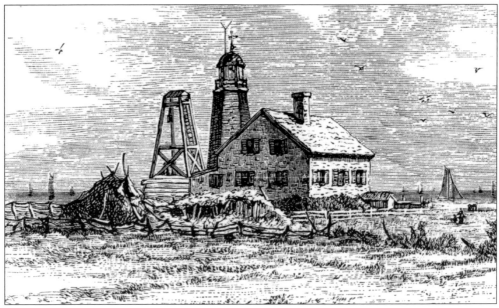

Pictured is an early engraving of the Stratford Point Light prior to 1880.

Acknowledgments

Although most of the images used in this book are from my own collection, I could not have put this volume together without the kind and able assistance of a number of individuals and institutions. First, thanks should go to my dad, Kenrick A. Claflin, who passed on to me his love of history, his integrity, and the tradition. Thanks should go especially to "Red," who lights up my life and makes it all worthwhile. Thanks also to Joshua, Jamie, Gram, Pat, Melissa, Ryan, and Kim.

I would like to thank Ralph and Lisa Shanks for their continued support and the loan of their fine photographs. Thanks to Glenda Bourque Zalewski for her continued encouragement, to Judy O'Brien for her proofreading and many suggestions, and to Julie for her patience. I would also like to acknowledge Andy and Anita Price, maritime antiques dealers, for their friendship and encouragement and for the loan of photographs from their collection. As always, thanks should go to Ken Black of the Shore Village Lighthouse Museum, a true gentleman. Thanks also to head keep' Wayne Wheeler of the U.S. Lighthouse Society and Tim Harrison at the Lighthouse Depot in Wells, Maine. In addition, I would like to express my appreciation to the following individuals for the loan of additional photographs and information used in this book: Colin Mackenzie of the Nautical Research Centre in Petaluma, California; John Hutchinson; Raymond A. Herberger; Scott Price and Chris Haven of the U.S. Coast Guard Historian's Office; and William P. Quinn. Also a special acknowledgement to Dick Boonisar, Gordon Benoit, Neil Janson, Steve and Carol Elve, John Koster for some wonderful Revenue Cutter Service photographs, Steve Marthouse and Joe Kiebish for some wonderful Coast Guard images, and Joe Lebherz of the Maritime Research Center.

My sincere appreciation to you all. You were most kind and generous and took the time when I asked. Finally, I would like to express my sincere gratitude to all of the lighthouse keepers, lifesavers, and Coast Guard personnel and their families, both living and past, for their unending devotion to duty—they all have set the standards.

INTRODUCTION

For over a century, more than 80 lighthouses, lightships, and lifesaving stations have guarded the Rhode Island and Connecticut coast—from Quicksand Point, Rhode Island, in the north to the Byram River in the south at the juncture with New York. Whether marking locations in fog and stormy weather or rescuing a ship's crew, these remote stations served innumerable vessels throughout their existence. Today, the sentinels that remain still remind us of the sacrifices of their crews and of the close ties that still bind us to the history of the New England coast. Cruising by the stately Penfield Reef Light, which rises 51 feet over the sea, you can easily imagine yourself back 100 years, pitting yourself against the elements. Seafaring today is not all that different than it was years ago.

The U.S. coast pilot for 1904 notes that in the "waters included between Point Judith and the East River [in New York] the chief obstacles to navigation are the fogs and the tidal currents. . . . The currents have considerable velocity in Block Island Sound, Fishers Island Sound and Long Island Sound. . . . Block Island Sound . . . shores are bold as a rule. Gardiners Bay is an excellent natural harbor. Fishers Island Sound has many dangers, and the currents have considerable velocity. Long Island Sound has many shoals lying along shore." Fogs, the dread of every navigator, are frequent in this region. Periods of thick weather and heavy gales, most common during the winter, may occur at any time. Among the islands of Narragansett Bay are Aquidneck, Conanicut, and Prudence, which are rather large and are covered with cultivated fields and groves of trees. Westerly from Point Judith is a continuous line of beaches, behind which are numerous salt ponds. The shore here is low and grassy but gradually rises to wooded lands some distance back. Conversely, the coastline of Connecticut is rock-bound and rugged, with numerous sandy beaches and occasional salt meadows. The many boulders, rocks, and ledges along the coast require the closest attention of the navigator because they often rise abruptly from deep water. Farther south, the coast has become developed with seaside resorts, parks, and bathing beaches.

Connecticut and Rhode Island, with their historic ports and sandy beaches, have attracted thousands of visitors for more than 100 years and have always derived much of their goods and income from their extensive coastal commerce. Mariners relied heavily on a system of navigational aids and lifesaving services to guide them safely as commerce increased. Think of the history of these beautiful stations: New London Harbor Lighthouse, the first light to be built on Long Island Sound; Falkner Island Light, where Keeper Oliver Brooks was credited with assisting more than 70 vessels in distress; the storm-swept New Shoreham Life-Saving Station on Block Island; Lime Rock Light, where Keeper Ida Lewis attained an enviable record of rescues during her career there; and Bartlett Reef Lightship, where their vessel was carried off station by ice on four occasions. These stately sentinels have become synonymous with safety and security. Just as Americans have always held a fascination for the sea, so too have they admired the men and women who worked to maintain our lighthouses and lifesaving stations. These devoted men and women who tended the lighthouses and patrolled the beaches gained a reputation for their heroism and steadfastness that survives today.

Coastal travel, however, was not always as reliable and safe. As numerous shipwrecks occurred off the coasts with startling losses during the Colonial years, each of the 13 colonies began to establish lighthouses and other navigational aids according to their needs. The first lighthouse in the colonies was lit in Boston Harbor on Little Brewster Island in 1716. However, as time went on, the need for more beacons was realized and additional lights were established at Brant Point on Nantucket (1746), Beavertail (1749), and at New London (1760).

At about the same time that the colonies were realizing a need for navigational aids, the citizens of neighboring Massachusetts (and later New Jersey and New York) were becoming more concerned with the incidence of shipwreck and loss of life along the coast. Although a coordinated system of lighthouses and lightships helped many mariners find their way clear of treacherous shoals and sandbars, the inevitable shipwreck did occur as the fog and New England weather forced ships ashore with repeated loss of life. Sometimes shipwrecked sailors were able to make their way ashore, only to perish from lack of shelter on desolate beaches.

In Massachusetts, prominent citizens of the day were beginning to appreciate the need for a system of shelter and rescue for mariners driven ashore and, in 1785, the Massachusetts Humane Society was founded. This organization created the foundation for what would become a coordinated system of rescue from shipwreck. Based on the British model, the Massachusetts Humane Society soon began to establish huts of refuge and lifeboat stations along the shore. As maritime trade continued to increase, however, a still more efficient and coordinated system was needed.

Though slowly at first, the newly formed federal government realized that a larger and more coordinated system of lighthouses, lightships, and navigational aids was needed. In 1789, Congress finally acted to centralize the responsibility for all navigational aids under the federal government. During this period, however, economy of operation ruled over efficiency and caused American lighthouses to become some of the poorest quality in the world. As the public's concerns continued to be voiced, in the 1850s the new U.S. Light-House Establishment was formed under an administrative board, thus beginning an era of high quality and efficiency that would continue into the 1930s.

As the number of fatal shipwrecks increased, Congress appropriated funds to create a coordinated system of lifesaving in 1871. To head this fledgling service, Sumner Increase Kimball was appointed to take over as superintendent. This new organization would be known as the U.S. Life-Saving Service. In a short time, it would become a model service that would last for 45 years. Under Kimball's leadership, the service would boast an unprecedented record of rescues, service, and efficient organization. In 1915, the U.S. Life-Saving Service merged with the Revenue Cutter Service to continue their fine record as the Coast Guard.

Although many of the early lighthouses and lifesaving stations no longer exist today, their stories remain forever in the hearts of seafarers and in the memories of the families that served as their guardians. These remote locations were more than job sites—they were home to the men and their families who served there. Indeed, many of the families who had to maintain the lights would be called upon to perform spectacular rescues when the keepers were caught away during storms. Through the wonderful photographs that remain today, we can get a glimpse into the everyday life of these men and women. As you turn these pages, please think of these dedicated people and the standards of excellence that they set. Enjoy the voyage.

One

THE EARLY YEARS

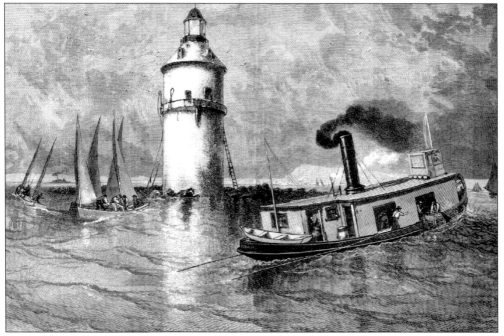

The study of the U.S. Light-House Establishment and American lifesaving services presents a wealth of activities and information that draws the student through more than 250 years of history. In the early years, before the American Revolution and the organization of a centralized federal government, the services provided were haphazard at best. The few lights for navigation that did exist might be installed by a group of sea captains who realized the need but lacked an organization charged with the responsibility. In the 1700s, the state governments began to establish some beacons in strategic locations after being put under sufficient pressure from ship owners and merchants. The few lighthouses that did exist were poorly constructed and maintained. By the 1790s, it was becoming apparent that the system of lights in the country was inadequate and greatly inferior to most other maritime nations. One of the first acts by the newly formed federal government was to take over control of the lighthouses in the former colonies, forming the basis of the country's lighthouse system. Pictured is an artist's rendition of the newly constructed New Haven Southwest Ledge Lighthouse from *Frank Leslie's Illustrated*, December 13, 1879.

Following standard practice in the early 1800s, the president of the United States and the secretary of the Treasury made the appointment of lighthouse keepers based on the local recommendation of influential public officials. This system of political patronage, common at the time, compounded the problem of obtaining the most qualified keepers for our lighthouses. Following presidential elections, the changes made to the staffing of the White House often affected the employment of the nation's light keepers. According to early records, keepers served for a few years, only to be replaced after an election, sometimes returning after their political party returned to office. These frequent upheavals resulted in lighthouses manned by poorly trained and unskilled people. As time went on, mariners were becoming displeased with the system. Occasionally, a sea captain would approach a landfall to find a lighthouse unlit, abandoned, or emitting a poor-quality beam. Shown is a c. 1847 letter from the secretary of the Treasury, detailing complaints against the keeper of Rhode Island's Dutch Island Light. (Author's collection.)

By the mid-1840s, mariners and ship owners began to exert pressure on Congress to recognize the need and importance of an organized system of navigational aids. Soon the government enlisted engineers to study the existing system and, in 1852, this board issued a comprehensive 760-page report on the subject. One of the primary recommendations would be the appointment of an independent board to organize a new system of aids to navigation.

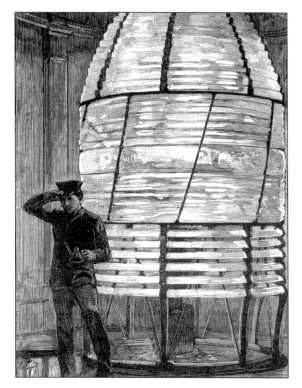

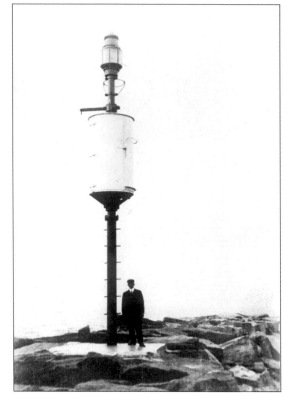

With the adoption of this new U.S. Light-House Board, a system of coordination and order was finally brought to the lighthouses and navigational aids in the country. Many new lighthouses, range lights, beacons, lightships, and buoys were constructed. Some older stations were moved to better serve the area, and maintenance was improved on the stations that remained. Experiments in fog signaling were conducted, and more modern light vessels were also added. As new programs were instituted to study and improve the equipment in use, the incidence of shipwreck slowly began to show signs of stabilizing. Shown in this c. 1900 photograph is the Point Judith Main Breakwater Center Light.

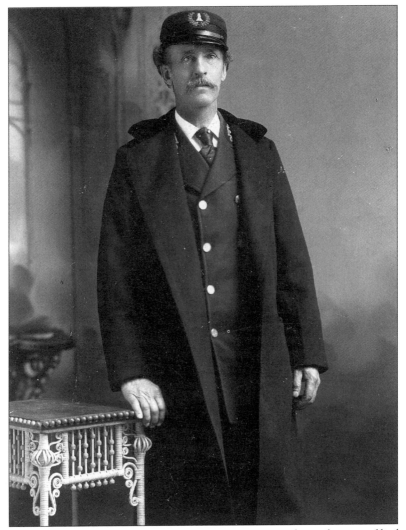

Under the former system of lighthouse management, training and morale were of little concern to local superintendents. For years the overriding emphasis had been placed upon economy of operation. One of the most important goals of the new U.S. Light-House Board was the improvement of the personnel administration and thus the improvement of the morale within the organization. Experience and ability would now become a determining factor in keeper appointments. Soon, as the working conditions improved, so did the keepers' lives, and many would begin long careers within the organization. Lighthouse keepers became important and respected people, with many serving up to 50 years. However, with this new organization came a strict attention to detail. Rules now required keepers to be neatly and completely uniformed, and inspections were made by the district inspector to ensure that the station was in good order. Brass work was to be kept polished and the lens and lantern spotless. Indeed, even pencils and paint brushes were now required to be accounted for. The keepers, however, were simply happy to be a part of the organization. They wore their uniforms proudly and with dignity, as many photographs of the day suggest. In this c. 1880 image, you can just see the insignia on this keeper's collar. The letter K within the insignia indicates that he is the principal keeper, with assistants having a number 1 or 2. Note also the U.S. Light-House Establishment insignia embroidered on his hat. (Sullivan Brothers photograph; author's collection.)

The first lights that guided mariners along the coast consisted of bonfires or crude towers supporting a wood- or pitch-fed flame. Sometime later, tallow candles were tried but, by the 1820s, the federal government began using a lantern fueled by whale oil. The lantern was fitted with a glass magnifying lens designed by Winslow Lewis. As the 1850s approached, and with the advent of improved glass optics invented by Augustin Fresnel, the U.S. Light-House Board began to refit America's lighthouses with an improved and more powerful Fresnel lens arrangement.

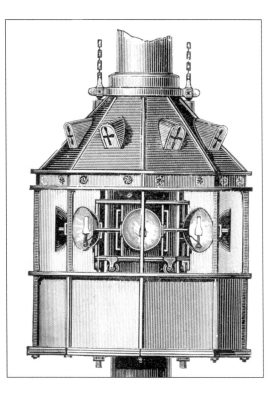

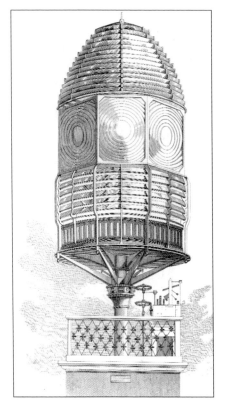

The U.S. Light-House Board continued to experiment with new methods of lighting. By the 1870s, new lamps and different types of oil and fuel began to be developed. One of the most important advancements adopted by this board was the new lens apparatus invented by Frenchman Augustin Fresnel. This arrangement of glass prisms, which concentrated the lost rays of light from the oil lamps into a powerful beam, would revolutionize the U.S. Light-House Establishment.

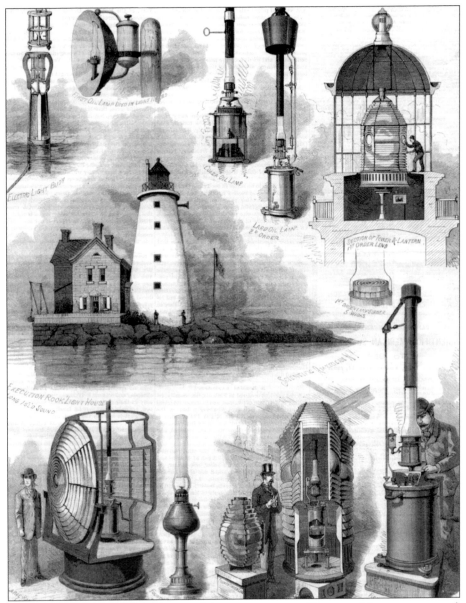

In this illustration, note the evolution of the various types of lamps and lens apparatus—from the early oil lamp with a parabolic reflector to the lard oil lamp, the fourth-order oil lamp, the incandescent oil vapor lamp, and the electric lamp used in the buoy. In 1902, the U.S. Light-House Board issued a complete set of instructions to light keepers. In these instructions, the board directed: "All keepers at light-stations shall wear a uniform in accordance with the uniform regulations issued by the Board. The utmost neatness of buildings and premises is demanded. Lights must be lighted punctually at sunset, and must be kept burning at full intensity until sunrise. The lens and the glass of the lantern must be cleaned daily and always kept in the best possible condition. Utensils of all kinds must be kept in their proper places. The revolving clockwork must be kept carefully from dust. The chariot or carriage upon which the lens revolves must be carefully wiped and the rollers properly oiled." (*Scientific American*, June 11, 1892.)

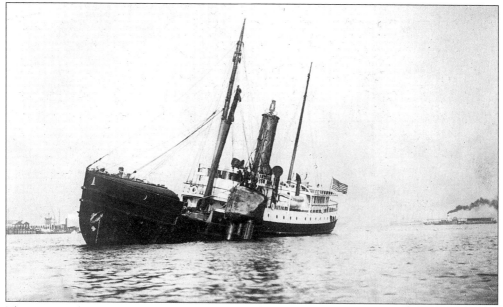

The U.S. Light-House Board organized the country into 15 lighthouse districts, each with depots to supply the lighthouses. Connecticut and Rhode Island constituted the Third Lighthouse District, and the depots included Goat Island in Newport Harbor and New London. From these depots, lighthouse tenders would service the light stations and perform other maintenance. Tenders were all named for flowers, including the *Iris*, *Gardenia*, *Mistletoe*, *Nettle*, *Daisy*, and *Tulip*. Note the U.S. Lighthouse Service emblem on the bow of the *Tulip*, shown at Point Judith c. 1900.

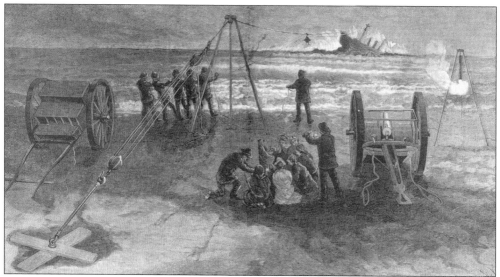

The establishment of lifesaving services to rescue and provide succor for shipwrecked sailors dates back more than 200 years. In the 1780s, the Massachusetts Humane Society first attempted to provide relief for victims of shipwreck by erecting huts for shelter along the Massachusetts coast. Later, the first lifeboat station was erected at Cohasset and, by the 1840s, others were erected and fitted out with boats, mortars to fire lines aboard vessels, and other apparatus. But still more was needed. (*Scientific American Supplement*, February 6, 1892.)

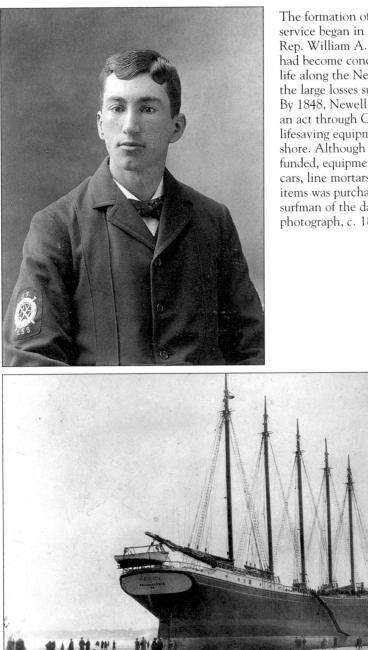

The formation of a national lifesaving service began in the 1840s. Rep. William A. Newell of New Jersey had become concerned for the loss of life along the New Jersey coast and by the large losses suffered by ship owners. By 1848, Newell was working to steer an act through Congress providing for lifesaving equipment for the New Jersey shore. Although no stations were funded, equipment such as metal life cars, line mortars, surf boats, and other items was purchased. Shown is a young surfman of the day. (Rankin Studios photograph, c. 1880.)

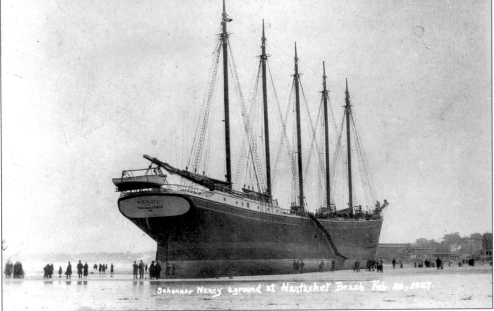

Schooner Nancy aground at Nantasket Beach Feb. 20, 1927.

As shipwrecks increased, so too did the cry for federal lifesaving stations in the country. At this time, the crews were still volunteer, gathered as needed from the local seafaring population. The stations were fitted with iron surf boats, mortars, and other necessary equipment, but it was decades before a nationwide system was put in place. Soon thereafter, the first lifesaving stations were constructed along the coast of New Jersey under the jurisdiction of the U.S. Revenue Cutter Service.

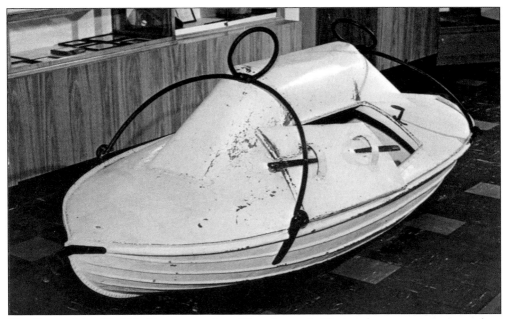

The Francis Metallic Life-Car was a unique lifesaving craft. During the most extreme weather, the life car proved a foolproof appliance for bringing survivors of wrecks to shore where the vessel was in reach of lifesaving mortars. The metal life car was a cigar-shaped craft, designed to be hauled along a hawser, back and forth between a wreck and the shore. Although eventually replaced by the breeches buoy, the life car proved its merits in numerous rescues. On the life car's first trial, volunteers were successful in rescuing over 200 people from the wreck of the ship *Ayrshire*.

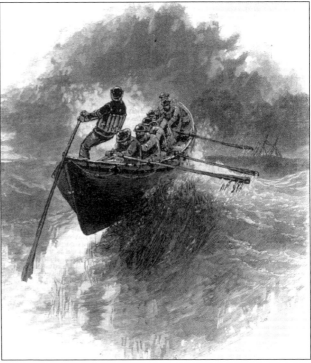

For some time, the lifesaving efforts continued under the volunteer system. However, without a keeper in charge to ensure that equipment was maintained, seamen continued to perish for want of equipment and trained lifesavers. In his paper "A Legacy: The United States Life-Saving Service," Dennis Noble notes that one town "used its lifeboat alternately as a trough for mixing mortar and as a tub for scalding hogs." This and similar failures proved the doom of such volunteer systems.

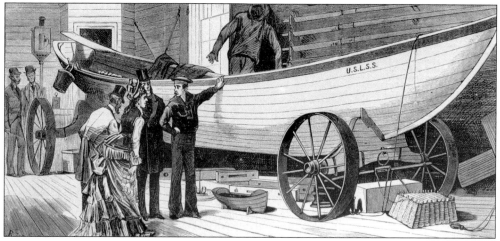

In 1854, Congress passed an act that would establish new stations along the coast of Long Island and New Jersey. The act also provided for full-time keepers, paid at $200 per year, and provided the funds for two superintendents to supervise the stations in the area. Crews, however, remained volunteer and would have to be gathered in the event of a wreck. (*Historical Register of the Centennial Exposition*, 1876.)

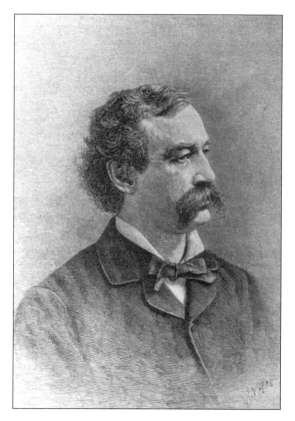

Sumner Increase Kimball was soon appointed as the U.S. Life-Saving Service's general superintendent. Due to Kimball's integrity and perseverance, the early years of the U.S. Life-Saving Service set the tone for many years to come. Under his expert management, this service became a model of efficiency and honesty and enjoyed a fine reputation. Its record of rescues and lives saved became second to none. (*Harper's New Monthly*, February 1882.)

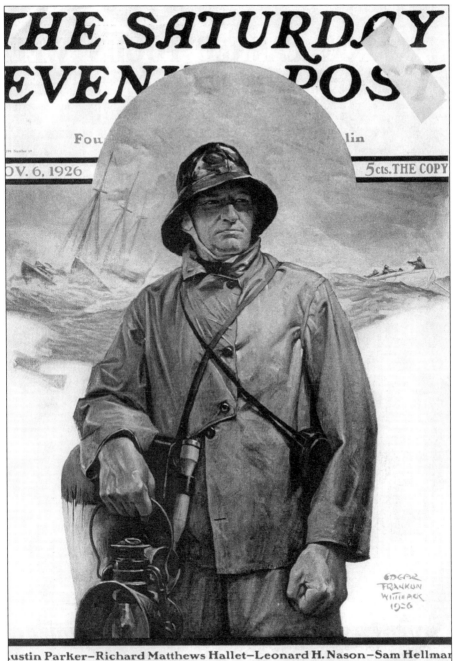

THE SATURDAY EVENING POST

Fou   lin

NOV. 6, 1926   5cts. THE COPY

EDGAR
FRANKLIN
WITHARK
1926

ustin Parker—Richard Matthews Hallet—Leonard H. Nason—Sam Hellman
Britten Austin—James W. Bellah—Chester T. Crowell—Octavus Roy Cohen

As the 1870s approached, the U.S. Life-Saving Service began to expand its line of stations along the coast. From an occasional house of refuge or boat station manned by dedicated volunteers, Kimball began to add new stations manned by paid, well-trained crews. By 1910, the Third District (the Connecticut and Rhode Island coast) boasted nine stations, many spaced four to six miles from the next or located in areas of particular need. These additional stations soon began to pay dividends as the tragic toll from shipwrecks stabilized and then fell for the first time in years. (*Saturday Evening Post*, November 6, 1926.)

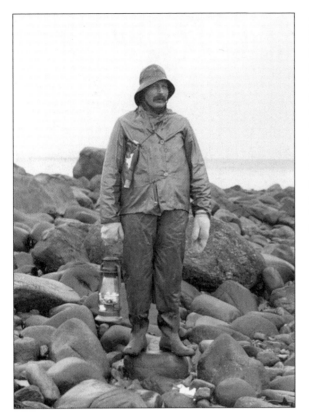

Each lifesaving station was manned by a keeper in charge and a crew of from five to eight surfmen. These men would be constantly drilled by the keeper in order to achieve peak efficiency. Each day and through the evening, surfmen would be required to maintain daily watches for vessels in distress from the station's watchtower and to patrol the beaches by night. When a wreck was spotted, the surfman would ignite his red Coston signal flare to alert the tower watchman and to signal the survivors that help was on the way.

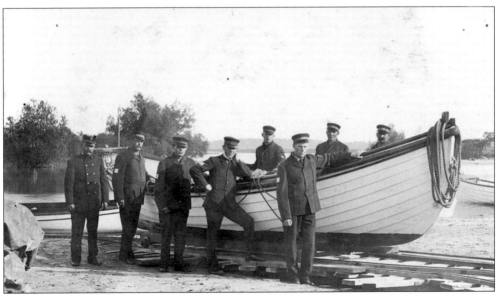

When a wreck was spotted, it would be the responsibility of the station keeper to decide how best to make the needed rescue. The three methods of rescue at the keeper's disposal would usually be the breeches buoy, life car, or surf boat. Using a surf boat (shown here) would be the usual choice when the vessel was over 600 yards from the beach. (Courtesy Steve Marthouse collection.)

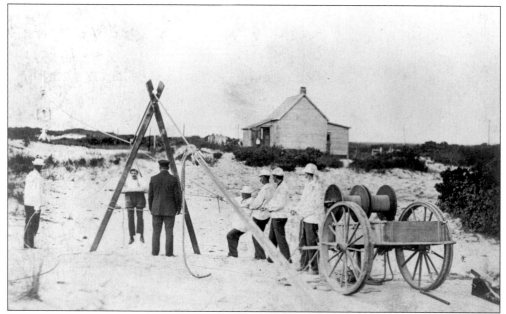

When the wreck was within 600 yards from the beach, the breeches buoy would be chosen. The surfmen would harness themselves to the apparatus or would occasionally borrow nearby horses to assist in the long pull down the beach. On the beach cart were coiled reels of shot line, heavy hawser, sand anchors, lanterns, as well as faking boxes to keep the coiled line from tangling.

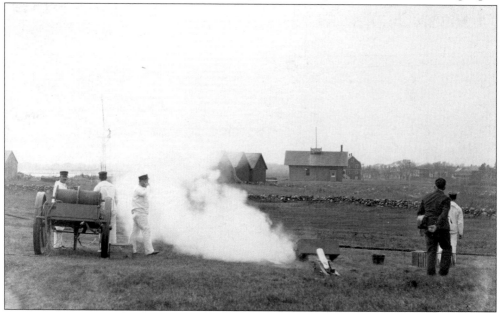

To gain access to the vessel with a line, a Lyle gun (a small bronze canon) was used to fire an iron projectile trailing a small shot line into the vessel's rigging. Surfmen, who were adept at judging winds and seas, were able to direct the projectile with great accuracy. Sailors on the stricken vessel would use the shot line to haul aboard the larger hawser and make it fast on the ship's mast. A life ring, with attached canvass pants or breeches buoy, was then sent out to pull the sailors to safety. (Clarence N. Trefry photograph, c. 1890.)

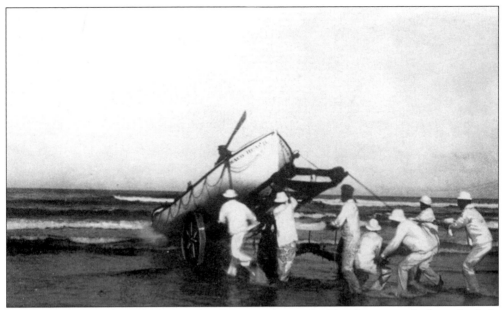

Often, the shipwreck would be too far offshore to be reached by the projectile from the Lyle gun. In such a case, the surf boat or lifeboat would be used. Weighing sometimes 1,000 pounds, the surf boat would be hauled on its four-wheeled carriage to a point on the beach suitable for launching. The keeper, most experienced in launching boats into the surf, would watch for the proper time and then direct his men to push the boat into the water, climb in, and begin to pull toward the wreck.

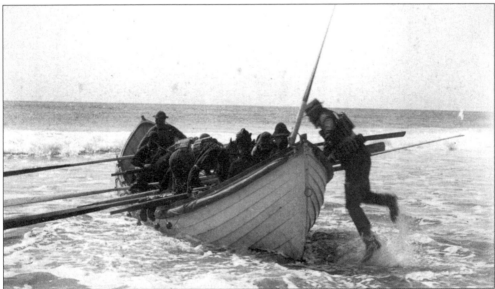

Once under way and after rowing for hours, the men would finally approach the wrecked vessel. The keeper, drawing on his years of experience, would approach the wreck in such a way to avoid being dashed to pieces while safely removing the sailors from the rigging. U.S. Life-Saving Service reports record numerous instances of crews laboring in excess of 24 and even 36 hours on end to effect such a rescue. Surf boats were often overturned or wrecked in the breakers once under way.

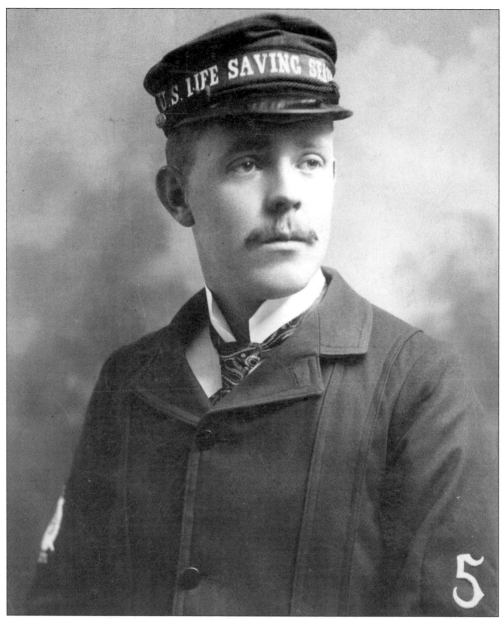

Over the years, many books—such as *Heroes of the Surf, Guardians of the Sea, Storm Fighters, Uncle Sam's Lifesavers,* and *Rulers of the Shoals*—have been written about the heroic lifesavers bringing hundreds of sailors and passengers from the sure death at the hands of the sea. Without hesitation, the crews would go out through hurricanes, blizzards, and the fiercest of seas. The U.S. Life-Saving Service built up a tremendous rescue record, though sometimes with the loss of their own men. The 1899 regulations of the U.S. Life-Saving Service (Article VI, Section 252) required that the men attempt the rescue and that the keeper "not desist from his efforts until by actual trial the impossibility of effecting the rescue is demonstrated." However, nowhere in the regulations did it say that the men had to return. Note the number 5 on this surfman's sleeve, indicating his seniority at his station. (Narragansett Studio photograph, c. 1880.)

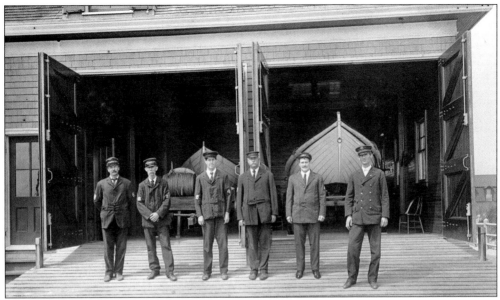

While on duty, surfmen constantly repaired and painted where needed and were always proud to pose for the camera. Here lifesavers take a break from their duties to pose in their dark winter uniforms at a New England station c. 1910. Just behind them are the station's two boats and the beach apparatus cart in the door to the left. Note, too, the numbers on the surfmen's sleeves, indicating their seniority.

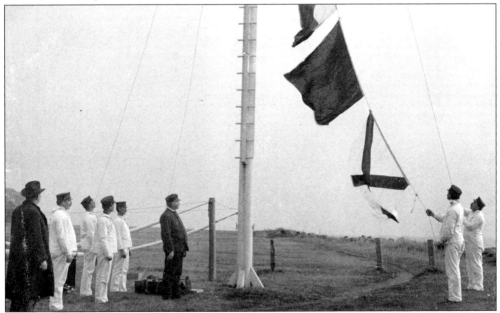

The U.S. Life-Saving Service regulations were quite detailed. Because of the nature of the work, it was most important that the men always be proficient at their tasks and be able to fill in at any position. Each day's activities were specifically laid out in the rules: Monday, station cleaning and maintenance; Tuesday, drill in launching and landing the surf boat; Wednesday, signal flag communications; Thursday, drill with beach apparatus and breeches buoy; and Friday, surf boat overturn drill. Saturday was for wash and Sunday for religious pursuits.

Two

BLOCK ISLAND AND RHODE ISLAND'S COASTAL LIGHTS

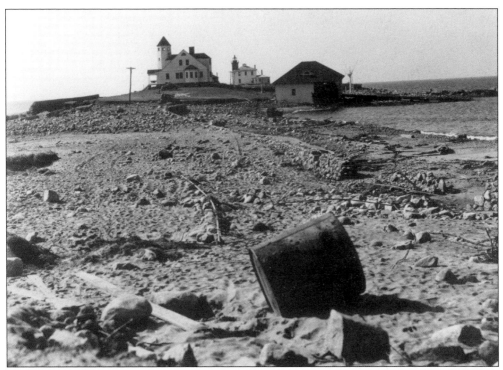

Block Island was first noted on charts in the early 1500s, but it derives its name from the Dutch trader Adrian Block, who explored Long Island Sound in 1614. The island is located 12 miles from the mainland and about 18 miles northeast of Montauk Point. Because of its distance from the mainland, its surface in the summer is cooled by a refreshing breeze, making it a wonderful summer getaway. However, the same characteristics that make it a refreshing summer resort have long buffeted residents with fearful winter gales, its shores assaulted with white billows of foam from the cold Atlantic. The island is about eight miles long and three miles wide, and it is doubtful if a more uneven landscape could ever be found. A noticeable feature of the island upon its discovery was its abundance of stone, a fact borne out in today's hundreds of miles of stone walls that the visitor can enjoy. Numerous pools and ponds, along with a seemingly inexhaustible supply of timber, made the island a haven during its early settlement. This c. 1938 image shows the Watch Hill Lighthouse and Coast Guard station. (Courtesy Coast Guard Historian's Office.)

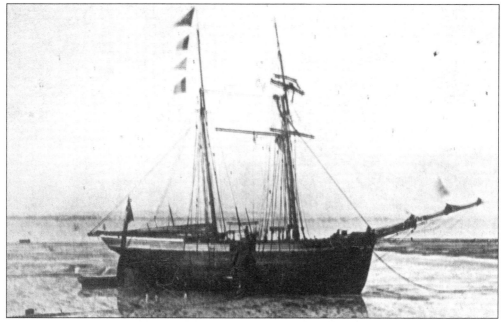

Block Island has been called "the island of a thousand shipwrecks," though surely many more vessels have met their fate off the shores of this charming island. Because of these alarming losses, work was begun early on beacons to provide guidance to passing mariners. The first lighthouse on Block Island was erected on Sandy Point, the northernmost extremity of the island, in 1829. The station consisted of two wooden towers that rose to 58 feet above the sea.

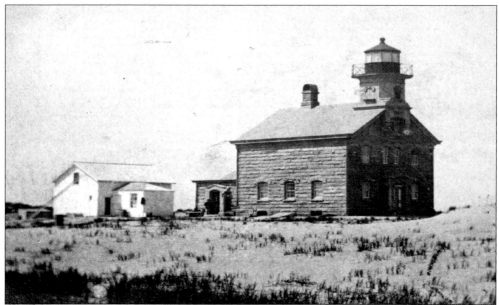

The two towers were attached to opposite ends of the keeper's dwelling, 25 feet apart. They each exhibited seven lamps with 15-inch reflectors. Because the station was exposed to the elements and the constant encroachment of the sea, it was rebuilt farther inland in 1837. By 1857, the sea again threatened the lighthouses and soon a new tower and dwelling was constructed at a cost of $9,000. The later 1866 light is shown c. 1870.

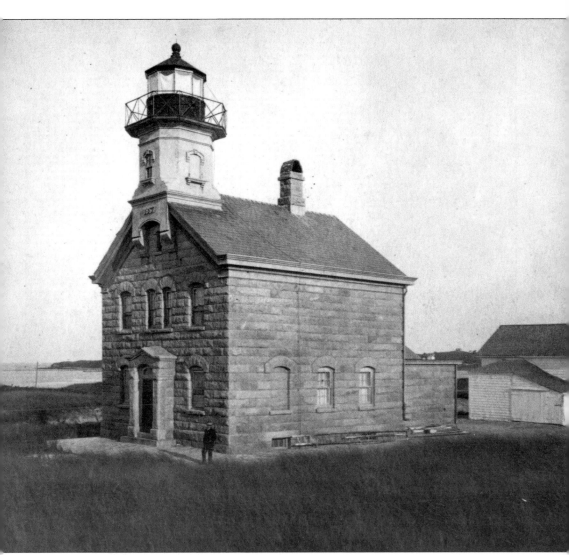

The new lighthouse on Sandy Point consisted of a single tower equipped with a fourth-order Fresnel lens, but again the sea began to threaten the structure. This fourth and last lighthouse on the site was constructed at a cost of $15,000. This striking example of period lighthouse construction consisted of a square light tower rising from the front roof of the keeper's dwelling, which was constructed entirely of brown-gray granite. Resembling a schoolhouse, the brown metal lantern atop the dwelling draws hundreds of visitors and photographers attempting to capture its singular charm and beauty. During the succession of lighthouses here, keepers held their positions according to the political winds of the time. Simeon Babcock, keeper from 1845 to 1849, was replaced by Edward Mott when Pres. Zachary Taylor took office. Likewise, Mott served until 1850, when Millard Fillmore took office. Such were the policies until the U.S. Lighthouse Service would see a complete reorganization in the 1850s. In 1955, the lighthouse was automated and, by 1970, was replaced with an offshore buoy. Today the structure has been lovingly restored to its original beauty and has become a worthwhile tourist stop. (Hacker photograph, c. 1870; author's collection.)

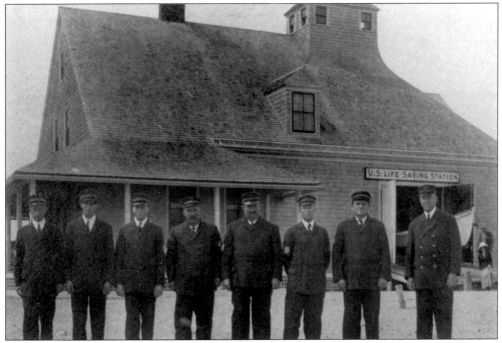

On the northernmost point of Block Island lies Sandy Point, at a point where the waters from Block Island Sound meet the open sea. Tidal currents here have considerable velocity, and Block Island Sound turns white with foam during a heavy gale. The lifesaving station at Sandy Point was constructed in 1898 and was the sixth in the country to be built in the Quonochontaug style. Note the station keeper on the right in this Coast Guard photograph. (Courtesy Ralph Shanks collection.)

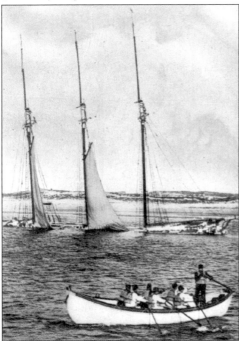

One of the worst shipping disasters of the day occurred on February 11, 1907, just off the North Lighthouse and within the range of the Sandy Point and New Shoreham stations. Just before 6 A.M., the keeper at the North Lighthouse was aroused by a knock on the door as survivors began to reach the shore. A short time before, the passenger steamer *Larchmont* had suffered a fatal collision with the schooner *Harry P. Knowlton*. Shown in a later photograph is the *Harry P. Knowlton* being surveyed by the Quonochontaug lifesavers.

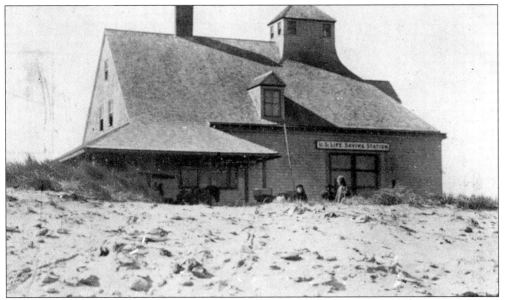

The collision between the *Larchmont* and the *Harry P. Knowlton* had cast hundreds of people into the frigid waters and carried many more into the depths as the two vessels sank. Men from the lifesaving stations, light keepers, and residents worked well into the following day to bring the more than 100 survivors to shore in a rescue effort remembered to this day. Shown in 1907 is the Sandy Point station as seen from the beach. (Courtesy Richard Boonisar collection.)

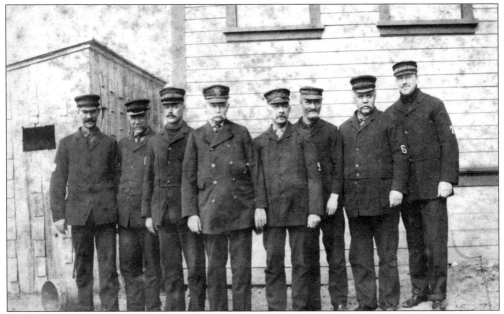

The first lifesaving station at New Shoreham was constructed in 1874 on the east side of the island near the boat landing. The station was one of 25 built from a standardized set of plans that considered functionality as well as a pleasing appearance. The stations were readily distinguished by their board-and-batten siding and abundant carved wooden ornaments, inspired somewhat by English Gothic church construction. Shown is the New Shoreham crew posing in 1904.

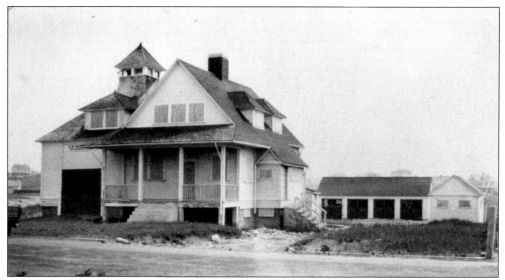

In 1898, as their space requirement increased, this Bibb No. 2–style replacement was built on the New Shoreham site. Shown is the station in 1941 under Coast Guard operation. Note the old boat room on the left. To the right is a later, larger boathouse constructed by the Coast Guard. As late as the 1960s, the 1874-type station was still in use on the site. In 1968, this early station was transported to the Mystic Seaport Museum, where it remains on display today. (Courtesy Ralph Shanks collection.)

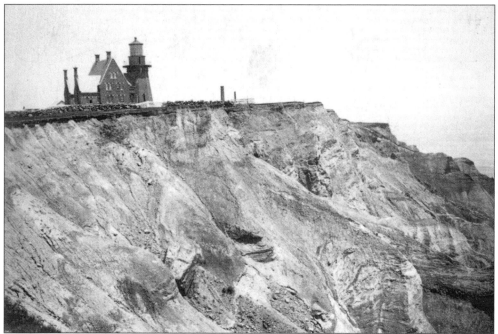

The second light station to be erected on Block Island was located on the southeast end of the island atop the tall bluff. Examining the steep bluff rising 152 feet from the sea, engineers found that this site would prove an ideal spot for the construction of the new light. Known as the Southeast (or New Shoreham) Light, this station was established in 1875 at a cost of $75,000. Note the intense erosion in this c. 1885 view by H.Q. Morton.

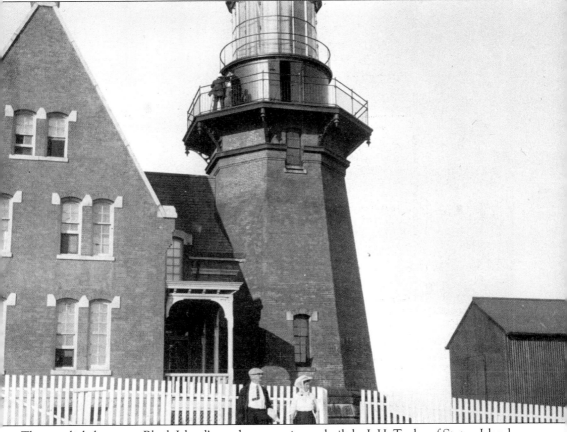

The new lighthouse on Block Island's southeastern tip was built by L.H. Taylor of Staten Island. It consisted of a two-and-a-half-story keeper's dwelling with an attached octagonal light tower. The Victorian dwelling accommodated two keepers and their families and gave this important station a lovely air of elegance. The light beam was produced by a large first-order Fresnel lens and could be seen for 35 miles. The light was first lit on February 1, 1875, and soon became a tourist attraction as the keepers patiently showed summer visitors into the lantern room. The first keeper was Henry W. Clark of Kingston, who was paid the moderate sum of $600 per year. His first assistant, Nathanial Dodge, received the sum of $450, and the second assistant received $400.

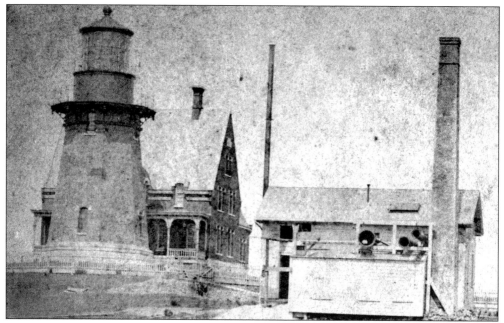

The fog signal was erected in 1874 and consisted of a first-class steam-powered siren. The signal was placed in its own brick structure located about 100 feet southeast of the light. The fog signal was powered by two four-horsepower, coal-fired steam engines (one acting as a spare). The sound was projected through immense trumpets protruding from the side of the building. This extremely early view shows the fog signal building under construction in 1874, with its tall chimney and fog trumpets.

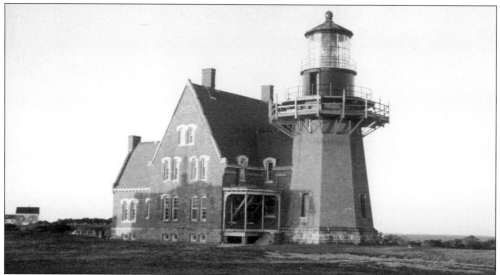

Faced with an ever growing erosion problem and the possible loss of this lovely structure, a group of volunteers was formed in the 1980s to raise funds to protect the light tower and dwelling. After considerable study, a plan thought impossible by many was instituted and funds were raised. By 1993, the International Chimney Corporation was working to move the 2,000-ton structure 360 feet back from the sea. Today, with the expertise of owner Rick Lohr and his staff of engineers, International Chimney has become the leader in preserving these historic structures.

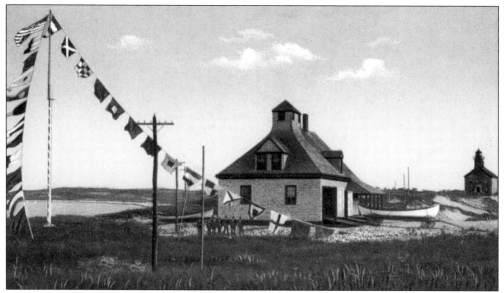

The Block Island Life-Saving Station was located on the west side of the island near Dickens Point. The first station there was constructed in 1872–1873. In 1886, this station was replaced with a more modern Bibb No. 2 type. In this view of the Sandy Point station, the crew is shown practicing with the International Code of Signal flags, a skill required of all members of the service.

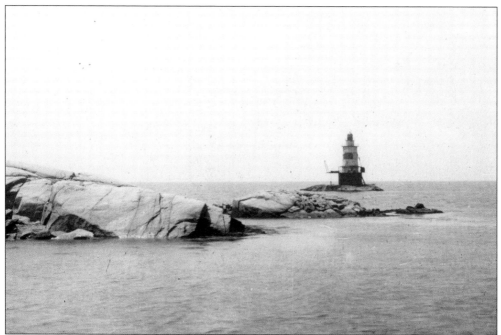

Sakonnet Point Light guards the east side of the Sakonnet River entrance to Narragansett Bay. Standing on Little Cormorant Rock, the white iron tower has marked this location since 1884. Life at this offshore light was difficult, with heavy seas often limiting access. Indeed one early keeper, upon first seeing his new assignment here, resigned his appointment after just a few moments in the lighthouse. The light tower still exists and can be seen from Sakonnet Point.

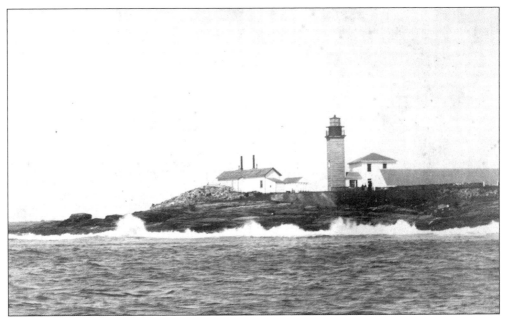

Beavertail Lighthouse was located on the southerly point of Conanicut Island in Jamestown, between the two entrances into Narragansett Bay. The first mention of a light in this area was as early as 1712, when merchants trading in the West Indies petitioned Congress for a light here. The first actual lighthouse here was constructed in 1748, but it was later destroyed by the British during the Revolutionary War. The square tower that we see today was built in 1856.

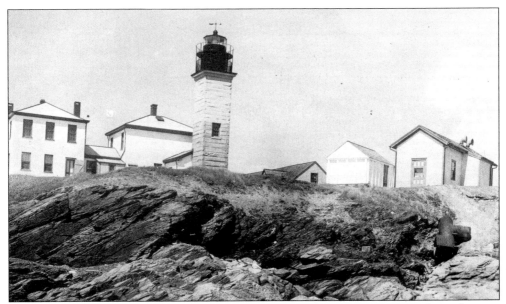

During its early years, Beavertail Lighthouse was known as the Newport Light and soon became an important site for testing new fog signal devices. Replacing its first hand-rung bell signal, inventor Celadon Daboll worked here to perfect his steam-powered fog trumpets, which soon became the standard for the U.S. Lighthouse Service. Note the fog signal trumpets protruding from the roof at the right in this July 4, 1924 view.

Castle Hill is a beautiful seaside promontory, lying on the east side of the Eastern Passage of Narragansett Bay. For years a light was needed here. Finally, in 1875, Congress appropriated the sum of $10,000 to construct the 25-foot tower. Serious difficulties were encountered in gaining a right-of-way to the light, and because of the landowner's continued complaints, the station's fog bell was discontinued in 1891. The tower has been white since 1899, displaying a flashing red light. (Courtesy Coast Guard Historian's Office.)

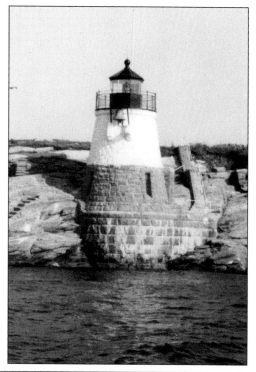

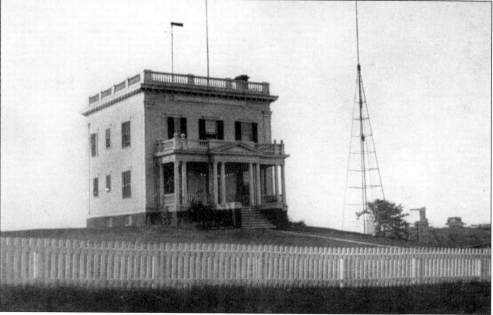

The U.S. Signal Service was organized to maintain communications with vessels at sea and to note and predict the development of storms. Signal Service stations were established in connection with lighthouses and lifesaving stations, where they were connected by telegraph. Such stations offered communications to ships at sea by light or flag, and later by radio. In time, this became our U.S. Weather Bureau, with stations across the country. (Rubin News Company view, c. 1910.)

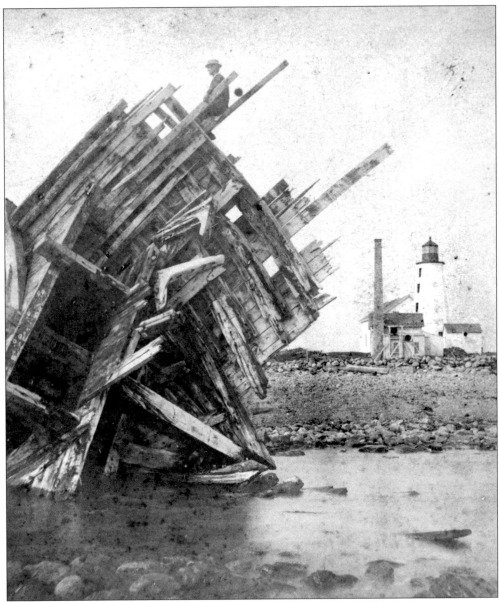

Point Judith lies at the junction of Narragansett Bay with the waters of Block Island Sound and has lacked protection for passing mariners for hundreds of years. Heavy fog and high seas are all too common to this area, and Squid Ledge just offshore has been the sight of numerous shipwrecks. As a result, Congress authorized the first lighthouse here in 1808. By 1810, a wooden octagonal light tower was erected and fitted out with lamps suspended by iron chains. In 1815, however, a hurricane swept the area, destroying the recently constructed station. In 1816, a new 35-foot white stone tower was built and equipped with 10 of the latest oil lamps with reflectors. During the early years here, life was extremely difficult, particularly during the winter. At times, family members were forced to sleep in front of the kitchen stove for warmth. By 1857, a new dwelling had been built. Shown in this c. 1880 view is the 1816 tower, flanked by the early fog signal building. Note the tall brick chimney for the coal-fired fog signal and the all too common remains of a shipwreck.

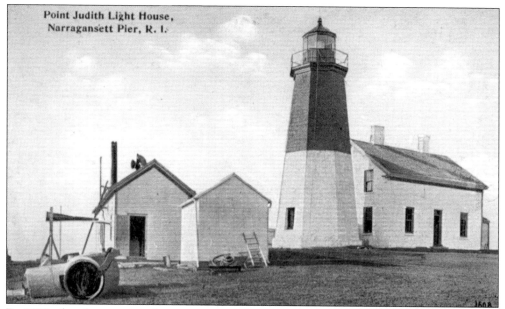

By 1908, the characteristic brown stripe on the upper half of the tower had been painted to distinguish this station from similar stations. The flashing white light continued from the 1857 fourth-order Fresnel lens, flashing every 15 seconds. The light was produced by incandescent oil vapor lamps until 1939, when it was converted to electricity. Note the three fog signal trumpets protruding from the fog signal building in this *c.* 1914 Charles H. Seddon view.

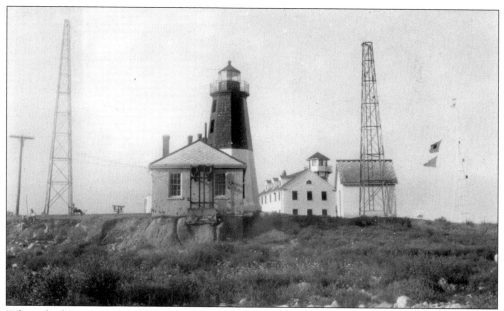

When the hurricane passed through in 1938, only the seawall was damaged. Later that year, the old 1875-type lifesaving station nearby was consumed by fire. In this 1939 view, the new Coast Guard replacement station can be seen behind the light tower. Note also the whole gale storm warning flags flying from the pole. Four combinations of two storm warning flags were used to notify mariners of impending foul weather.

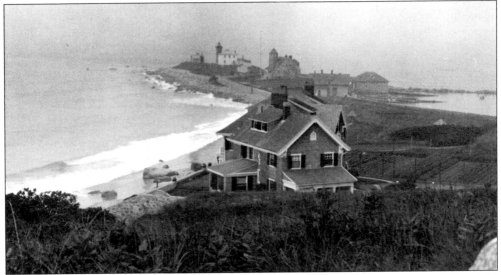

The first light shone from Watch Hill in 1807, on land purchased from George and Thankful Foster. This location has always been of particular importance for its proximity to Stonington Harbor (three miles to the north) and as a guide into the entrance of Fishers Island Sound. The colony of Rhode Island erected a beacon here in the 1700s, but it was destroyed some years later. Note the lighthouse and lifesaving station on the point in this c. 1920 view.

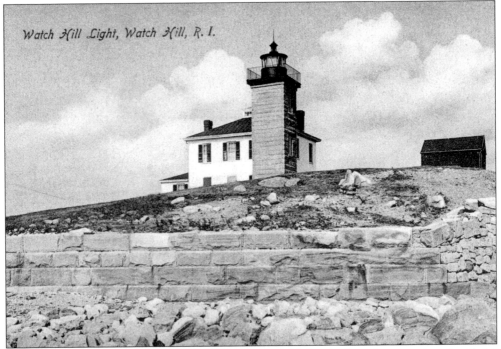

Watch Hill Light, Watch Hill, R. I.

The lighthouse was first constructed of wood. It was 35 feet high and was equipped with 10 lamps with reflectors that were hung on weight-driven rotating iron frames. Jonathan Nash, the first keeper, served for 27 years before retiring. By the 1850s, a new structure was needed and, in the mid-1850s, this 45-foot brick tower and attached dwelling were built. The house consisted of seven rooms and an oil storage area in the basement.

Between the 1890s and the 1920s, many local scenes were produced on china pieces for sale to tourists. These china pieces—ranging from plates and cups to creamers, pin plates, and napkin holders—featured scenes from all over the country. Today, U.S. Life-Saving Service scenes bring a premium and are most collectible. This Watch Hill Lighthouse commemorative vase dates from *c.* 1900. (Author's collection.)

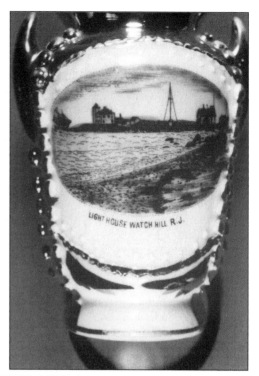

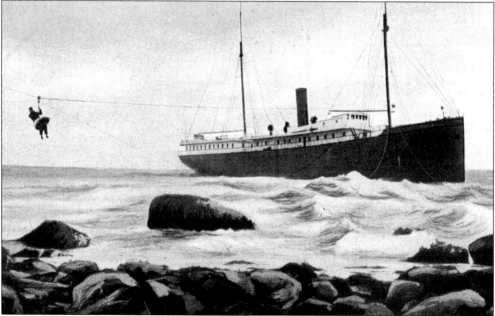

On March 19, 1905, the steamer *Spartan* came ashore in a fierce gale just two miles east of the Watch Hill Life-Saving Station. Upon discovering the vessel, the lifesavers launched their surf boat and were able to remove 11 of her crew. The master elected to remain on board with the remaining crew in hopes of working the vessel free. By daybreak, however, as the seas pounded the vessel, all hopes were abandoned. The remaining crew members were rescued by breeches buoy as the ship broke up. (*Rhode Island News* view, *c.* 1910; author's collection.)

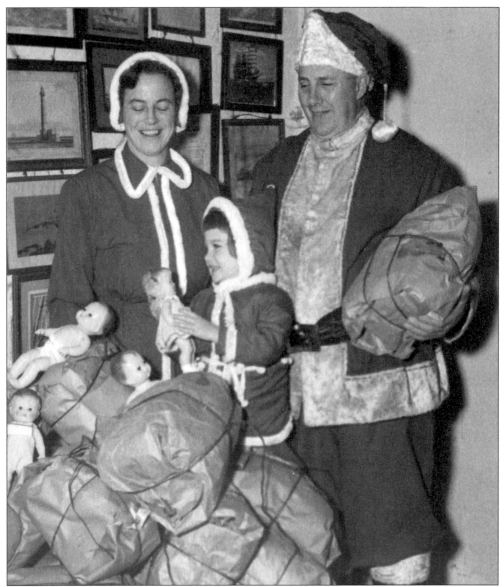

Author, lecturer, and historian Edward Rowe Snow has been credited with more than 100 books and pamphlets, as well as newspaper articles, lectures, and tours of the area. Snow was born in Winthrop, Massachusetts, and spent most of his life studying the lighthouses, islands, and legends of the New England coast. Snow and his wife, Anna-Myrle, made hundreds of visits to light stations throughout New England and considered the light keepers and their families to be extensions of their own family. Today, many consider Snow's interesting and readable accounts of life at these stations to have been the impetus that launched an increase in lighthouse interest and preservation. In this photograph, Anna (left), daughter Dorothy (center), and Edward Snow are getting packages ready for their well-known Christmas airdrops to remote lighthouses and Coast Guard stations. In 1926, Capt. William Wincapaw began the tradition of dropping Christmas gift packages from his plane to remote lighthouse families. Later, Snow would continue the "flying Santa" tradition, which is still carried on by local groups.

Three
NARRAGANSETT BAY

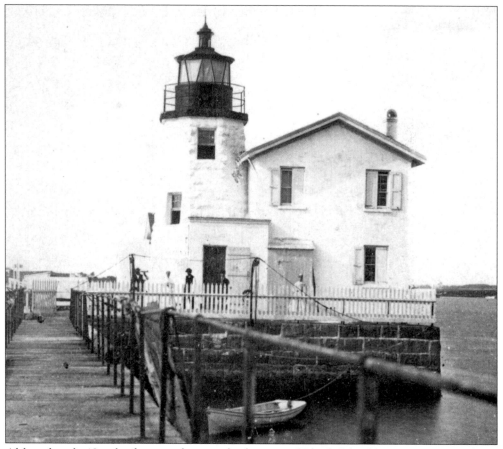

Although only 48 miles from north to south, the state of Rhode Island boasts over 400 miles of shoreline dotted with numerous small islands, bays, and inlets. Probably the most prominent feature on a map of the coast would be Narragansett Bay, lying between Point Judith on the west, Seaconnet Rocks on the east, and extending six miles northward to Bullock's Point. This lovely region is host to many important coastal towns and villages, not the least of which are Newport, Little Compton, Bristol, and Pawtuxtet. During its peak years, Narragansett Bay hosted no less than 29 of the state's 32 lighthouses. Newport was always an important port for domestic and foreign trade. As early as 1823, a lighthouse was established to mark the harbor entrance. The light tower was erected on the northern tip of Goat Island, where it remained until 1842, when a new station was built on the north end of the new breakwater making out from the island. The original tower was moved in 1851 to become the Prudence Island Lighthouse. This *c.* 1870 view was taken by A. Williams. (Author's collection.)

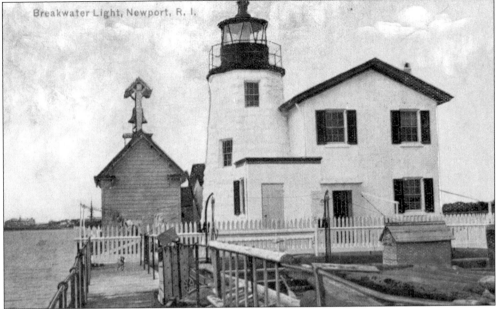

Breakwater Light, Newport, R. I.

Keepers continued to stay in the original quarters on the island until 1864, when this six-room dwelling attached to the light was constructed. This new light was first equipped with 15 oil lamps, each with a silvered reflector to produce the light beam. Fog machinery was installed in 1873 to strike the fog bell mechanically every 15 seconds. In this c. 1920 postcard view, note the fog signal building to the left, with the bell tower protruding from the roof.

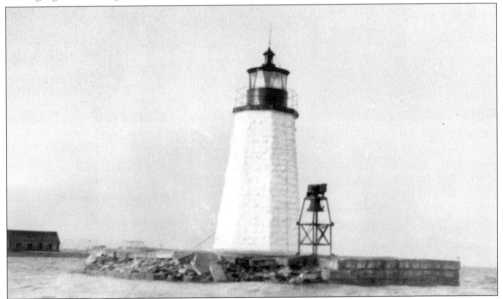

By the 1860s, the light was refitted with a fourth-order Fresnel lens. By 1908, the U.S. Light-House Board List of Light-Houses listed the light as displaying a sixth-order fixed red light visible for 10³/4 miles. The light here was electrified in the 1920s and was in time automated. Although the keepers are gone and the dwelling has been removed, the stone light tower remains today on Sheraton Hotel property and can be viewed with permission. (Courtesy Coast Guard Historian's Office.)

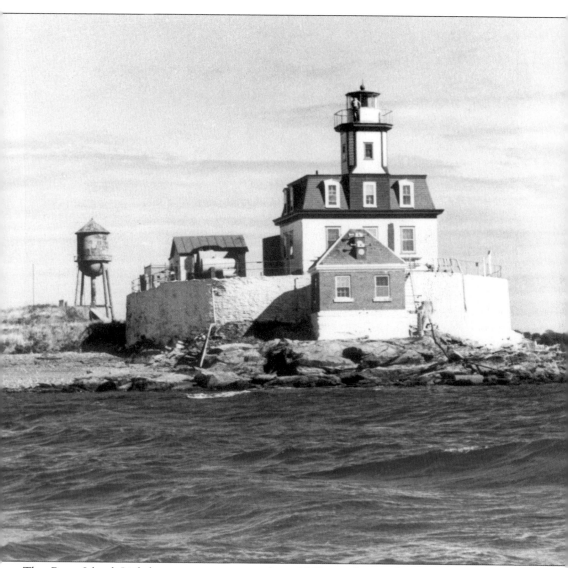

The Rose Island Lighthouse was constructed in 1869 on the southwest bastion of Fort Hamilton. The light here marked the east side of the Eastern Passage into the bay. The tall sixth-order lantern rises from a one-and-a-half-story, mansard-roofed structure atop the stone bastion. During the early years, portions of the property were used for the fort's ammunition storage, as well as a rifle range, which must have surely annoyed the keepers there. Keeper Charles S. Curtis served one of the longer terms (31 years). During his career, he earned two medals for the saving of lives. In the 1970s, the Newport Bridge made the lighthouse obsolete and, by the 1980s, vandals had all but doomed the structure. Soon, however, local volunteers began efforts to save the old station and formed the Rose Island Lighthouse Foundation. After years of fund-raising and thousands of hours of hard work by members of the foundation, the Rose Island Lighthouse is now a living museum, hosting hundreds of overnight visitors who come to be "keepers for the night." (Courtesy Coast Guard Historian's Office.)

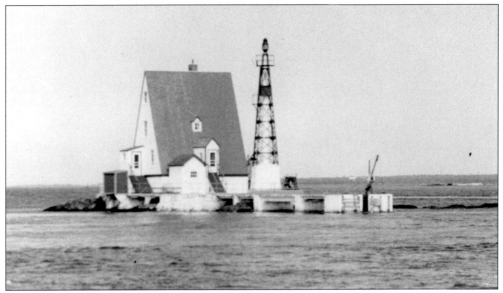

The light station on Gull Rocks, in the easterly entrance to Newport Harbor, is of a most unusual design. The A-frame dwelling was constructed in 1887 to exhibit two lights, one in each end of the building. In the east end was a fixed white light and in the west end a fixed red light—both from lens lanterns hoisted to the peak 42 feet above the water. In 1928, the lights were replaced by a skeleton tower, as seen in this *c.* 1940 Coast Guard photograph.

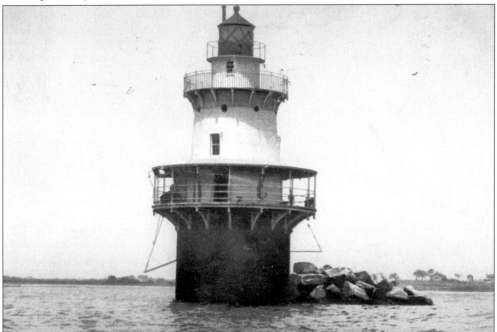

In 1901, the Hog Island Shoal Lighthouse was established to replace the Hog Island Shoal Light Vessel No. 12. This attractive light was located at the junction of Narragansett Bay and Mount Hope Bay. The light was a typical "spark plug" light, built of cast-iron plates and mounted on a concrete caisson. The station included a fourth-order flashing white light and a compressed-air siren for use in fog.

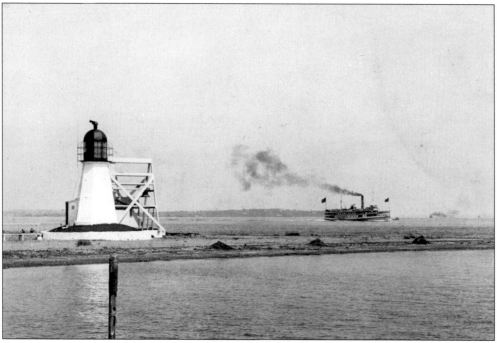

On the east side of Prudence Island lies Sandy Point, extending out into the bay, and the Prudence Island Lighthouse. The 25-foot white octagonal tower was originally constructed for the Newport Harbor (Goat Island) light but was moved to this site in 1851. Beside the light was an open skeleton tower supporting the fog signal bell. Just 200 feet inland was the six-room, one-and-a-half-story keeper's dwelling.

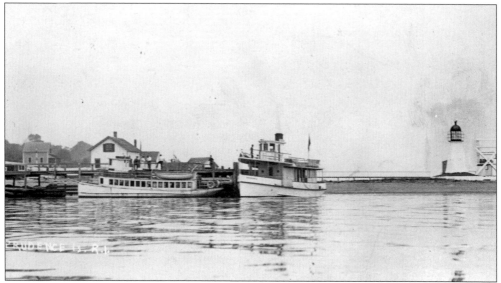

Seen on the left in this 1916 view is the dwelling of lighthouse Keeper Martin Thompson and his assistant George T. Gustavus. In 1938, as hurricane seas rose, the keepers sought refuge in their dwelling along with their families and guests. As the huge waves approached, the building crumbled. All of the occupants were swept away except for Gustavus, who was pulled to safety by local residents.

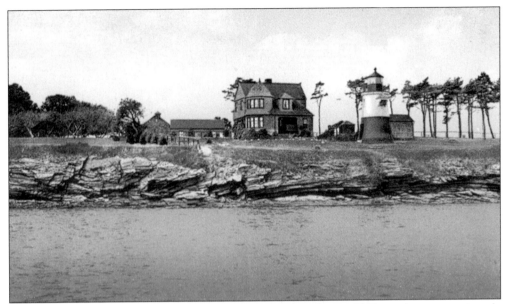

The government lighthouse on Gould Island was first lit in 1889, replacing a privately maintained beacon there. The station was located on the east side of the island and consisted of a conical brick tower that was painted white on the upper half and red on the lower half. Behind the tower was a lovely two-and-a-half-story keeper's dwelling. It was constructed of red brick on the first story, with the second story and roof finished in natural wood shingles. A Victorian turret and dormers completed the structure.

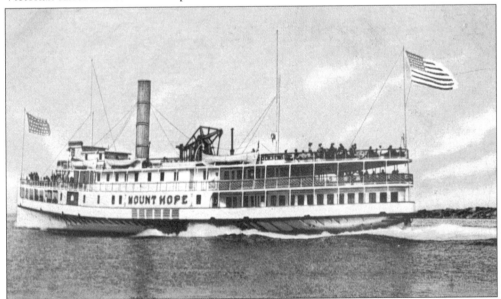

The latter half of the 19th century was the heyday for travel by steamships along the New England coast. One of the premier carriers during this period was the Eastern Steamship Company. The company's extensive fleet was made up of a large number of steamers, from the great steel express boats to the smaller connecting steamers. Steamers of the era were designed with comfort and convenience in mind and were well known for their excellent dining service. Shown c. 1910 is the steamer *Mount Hope* in Narragansett Bay.

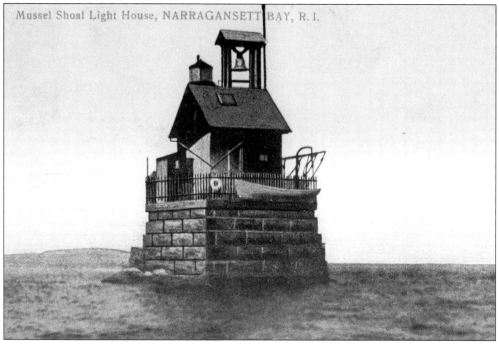

The Muscle Bed Shoals Light, an unusual-looking station, was located opposite the Bristol Ferry Light in the channel to Mount Hope Bay. The first light on this site was constructed in 1873 and consisted of a 12-by-12-foot red dwelling atop a square granite pier. Surrounding the house was an iron railing that left just a few feet of space for the keeper to walk. Atop the dwelling was a hexagonal tower equipped with a sixth-order Fresnel lens.

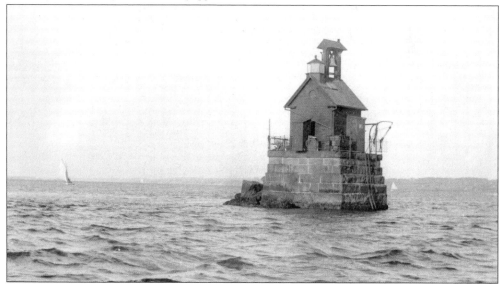

In 1879, the deteriorating light at Muscle Bed Shoals was rebuilt with a one-room dwelling on the same pier. On the roof was a frame supporting the fog bell and a sixth-order lantern showing a fixed red light. Walls and ceilings leaked constantly. Over the years, the U.S. Lighthouse Service attempted to make repairs, but to no avail. Finally, in 1939, the light was dismantled and replaced by a skeleton tower.

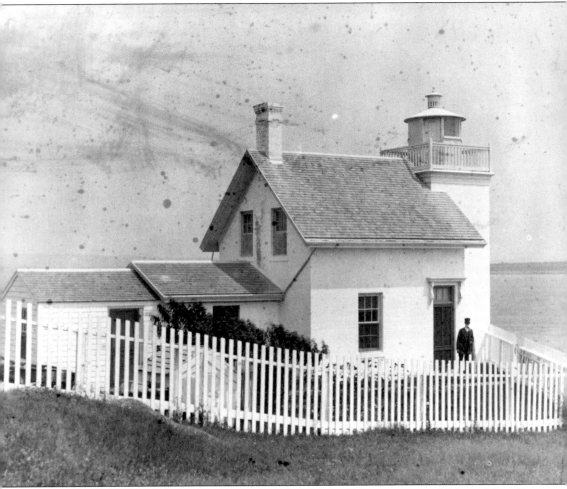

The town of Bristol is pleasantly situated on the waters of Narragansett and Mount Hope Bays and has always been a prominent town in the area. At one time, commerce in the area was extensive to feed its growing manufacturing facilities. However, the narrow passage between the two bays proved difficult, particularly during the night and during periods of heavy weather. A lighthouse was therefore needed to mark the passage. By 1854, a light was established on Bristol Ferry Point. It was equipped with a sixth-order fixed white light. The small square tower rose just above the roof of the dwelling and could be seen for more than 10 miles. Shortly after 1900, the lens was upgraded to a larger fifth-order lens, which produced a fixed white beam visible for 11 miles. Note the keeper, probably Edward P. Hoxsie, posed at the doorway in this 1884 view. (Courtesy Coast Guard Historian's Office.)

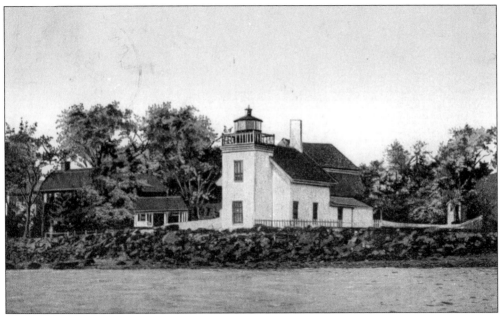

Bristol Ferry Light's only female keeper, Elizabeth Pearse, served here after her husband, head keeper George Pearse, passed away in August 1856. Unfortunately, she also passed away in 1857, after serving less than a year as keeper. The light was discontinued in 1927, and the lantern was later removed. Today the dwelling and the tower still stand, now in private hands, at the side of the Mount Hope Bridge.

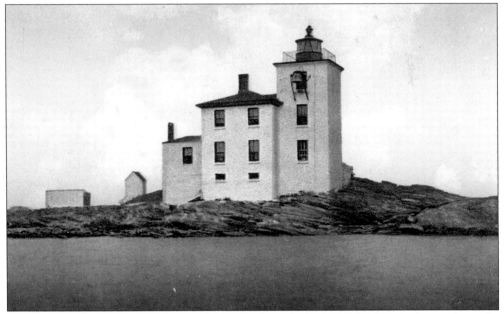

The Dutch Island Lighthouse lay on the southerly end of Dutch Island to guide vessels up the Western Passage and into the southern entrance of Dutch Harbor. The light was established in 1826 on six acres of land purchased by Gov. James Fenner for the federal government. Soon a stone tower and dwelling were constructed, equipped with a fixed white light generated by eight lamps.

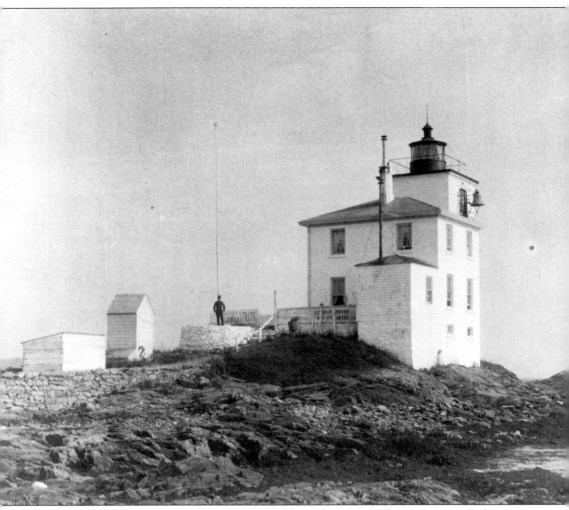

Like many light stations before the institution of the U.S. Light-House Board, the one on Dutch Island was poorly maintained—it leaked and eventually proved unlivable. By 1856, funds had been appropriated and the tower was reconstructed and fitted with new lighting apparatus. The lighthouse was located near Fort Greebe, a federal fortification there since the 1860s. In 1923, this proximity proved a blessing. While the keeper was away, a family member chose to burn brush piled behind the station. The day was windy, however, and soon the nearby field was ablaze, the fire spreading toward the buildings. Soon the men from the fort were assisting, though the variable winds continued to push the blaze throughout the area. The men were finally able to subdue the blaze with the loss of only one government storehouse on the fort property. Note the keeper standing beside the flagpole in this 1880s view. (Courtesy Coast Guard Historian's Office.)

Plum Beach Lighthouse stands in 17 feet of water on the northerly end of Plum Beach Shoal in the Western Passage of Narragansett Bay. The light was erected in 1897–1899 in response to complaints that steamers rounding Dutch Island in the fog had run aground on the opposite side of the channel. In the early years, qualified keepers were hard to retain because of the light's remote offshore location and the problems that arose getting to it during storms.

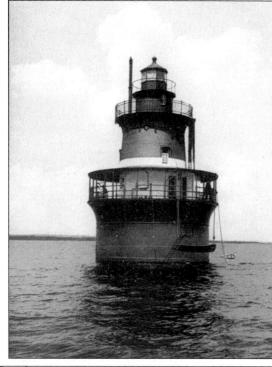

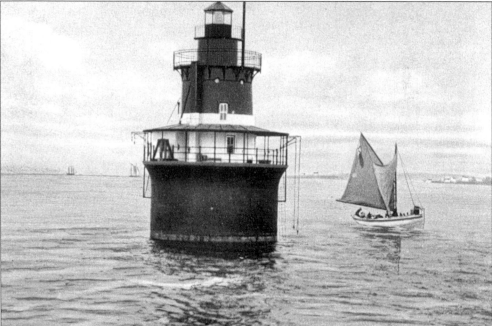

Soon after completion of the light, large cracks began to develop in the foundation caisson. Despite repairs in the 1920s, the cracks continued to weaken the structure. The Hurricane of 1938 aggravated the problem and caused extensive damage to the foundation, gallery, and landing. During the same storm, neighboring Whale Rock Light to the south was totally destroyed.

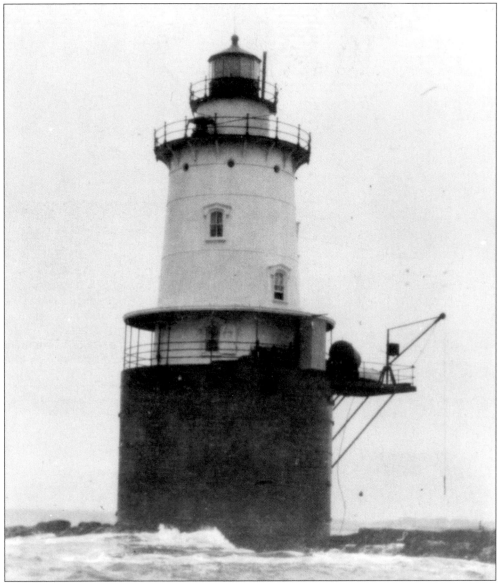

Following the wreck of the schooner *Pearl* on the reefs in the Western Passage into Narragansett Bay in the 1860s, sailors petitioned for a light to mark the reefs at Whale Rock. After years of failed appropriation requests, this white conical light tower was finally constructed on Whale Rock in 1882. Similar to other caisson-style lights in the area, life here was most remote and confining for the keepers. During the 27 years after completion of the light, 16 head keepers served on this station. On September 21, 1938, the winds began to pick up as the sky became dark. The head keeper had been ashore that day for supplies and, by afternoon, he was unable to return. Assistant Keeper Walter Eberle, left in charge of the light, continued his duties, but increasingly larger waves battered the structure as the day wore on. Late that afternoon, a wall of water (described by some as a tidal wave) struck the light. The force of the water tore away everything above the concrete base, washing the structure into the bay. Only the concrete base remained. Eberle's body was never recovered. (Courtesy Coast Guard Historian's Office.)

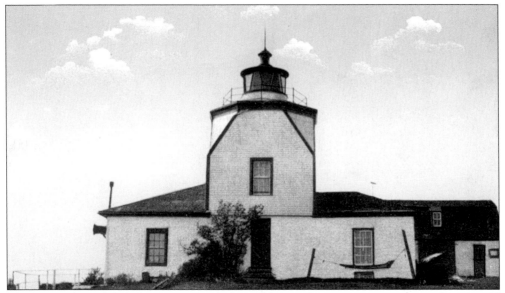

The Warwick Neck lighthouse consisted of an odd-shaped square tower constructed on the old keeper's dwelling, which was made of stone. The light is situated on land that once belonged to William Greene and was sold to the government for $750 in 1826. The light sits on the north side of the entrance to Greenwich Bay, guiding vessels with its white fourth-order light visible for 12 miles. The original tower required continual maintenance to keep the structure watertight.

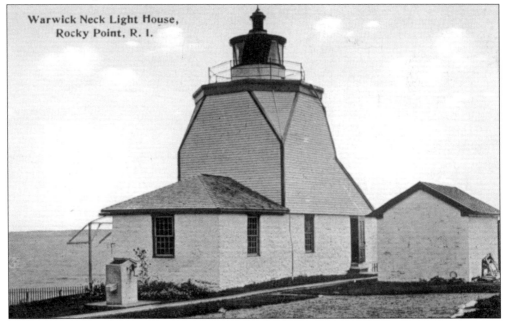

Warwick Neck Light House, Rocky Point, R. I.

Shortly after its construction, the outside of the tower was skim-coated with a lime-gravel mix and, some years later, was sheathed with wood. In 1832, a new keeper's house was erected to help solve the difficulties with water leaks. The house was rebuilt in 1888. In 1932, erosion forced the erection of a new steel tower, which was moved once again after the Hurricane of 1938. Today the light can still be seen just past Rock Point Beach.

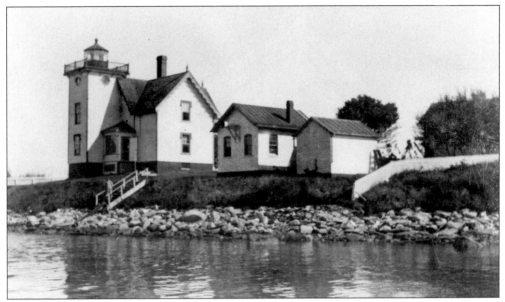

If you drive down North Bay View Drive on Conanicut Point in Jamestown, you will come across a lovely one-and-a-half-story Victorian dwelling at No. 64. If you look closely, you will notice a square two-story protrusion on the ocean side with a railing encircling its flat roof. This little dwelling is the original 1884 Conanicut Island Lighthouse. As shipping declined in the area, the light was discontinued in 1933 and the property was sold. (Courtesy Coast Guard Historian's Office.)

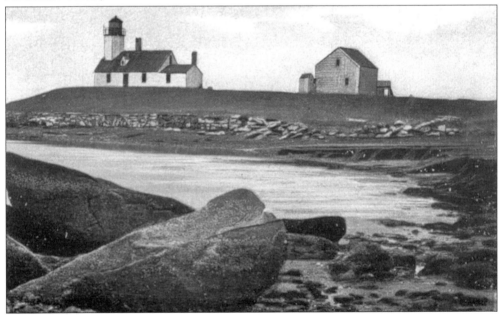

The lighthouse at Poplar Point was constructed in 1831, probably to mark shallow Wickford and North Kingstown Bays. The station consisted of a drafty one-story stone dwelling with an octagonal tower rising from the roofline. The keeper's access into the tower was through a small unfinished bedroom. Despite renovations to the tower in 1870, the U.S. Light-House Board decided to replace this station with a light offshore on Old Grey Rock in 1880.

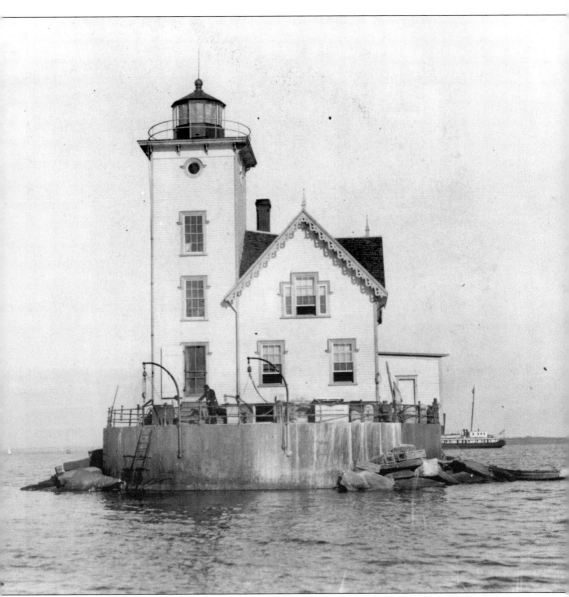

This new lighthouse to mark Wickford Harbor was completed in November 1882. This light better marked the entrance to Narragansett Bay and the route into Wickford Harbor. The station consisted of a fine eight-room Victorian dwelling, one and a half stories in height and constructed on a concrete caisson atop Old Grey Rock. Attached to the dwelling was the 50-square-foot, three-story, fifth-order light tower. Included on the station was a Stevens fog bell, struck by machine every 20 seconds during periods of fog. At times, keepers at this remote station suffered greatly from their isolation, cruel storms, and buffeting winds. Often the keepers and their families would be marooned for several weeks by storms and fog. Many times, supplies would begin to dwindle, forcing the keeper to attempt the trip in his small boat to the mainland. At the left center of this view, note the keeper inspecting the davits, which would raise and lower the station rowboat. (Courtesy Coast Guard Historian's Office.)

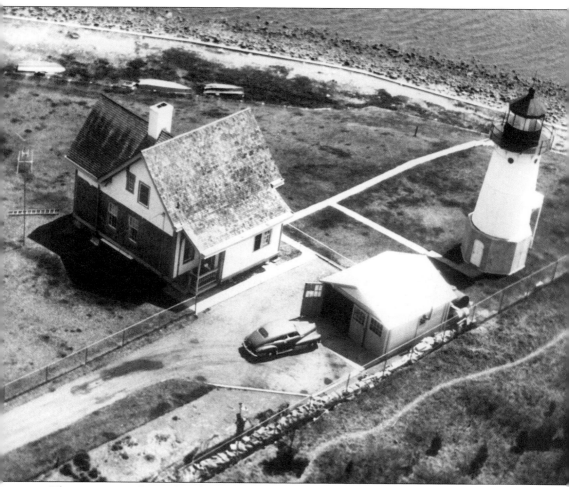

This interesting Coast Guard view shows the Warwick Neck lighthouse from the air in 1951. The station was located at the entrance to Greenwich Bay, and a light has been in operation here since 1826. The station affords a commanding view of Narragansett Bay. Despite numerous difficulties in maintaining the dwellings over the years, keepers have enjoyed the location. According to Robert G. Bachand in his book *Northeast Lights*, Keeper Elisha Case maintained a garden on the lighthouse grounds to supplement his family's meals. Upon his transfer in 1831, Case refused to leave the station until he was assured that he would be permitted to continue growing and harvesting his crop. The early keeper's dwelling proved quite damp, and its two 11-by-11-foot rooms were not adequate to house the keeper properly. A three-room addition was built in 1832. The dwelling lasted until 1888, when the structure was again replaced. In the 1850s, the old reflector lamps were replaced with a new fourth-order Fresnel lens and, in the 1930s, the station was electrified. Although automated in the 1980s, the station's green light continues to this day. This Coast Guard photograph was taken *c.* 1951. (Author's collection.)

Four

THE U.S. LIFE-SAVING SERVICE

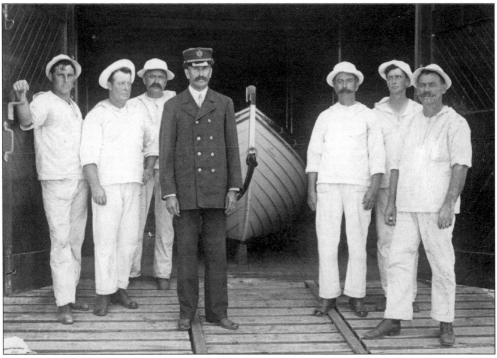

One of the worst gales ever to sweep the Rhode Island coast occurred in the late spring of 1909. Blowing from the west-southwest, the storm kicked up tremendous seas that sent combers rolling in on the shores from Watch Hill to Point Judith in huge masses, threatening to crush everything in their path. Shortly after 7 P.M., surfman Charles S. Larkin, who was on duty in the tower of the Quonochontaug Life-Saving Station, sighted three barges lying at anchor about six miles off the beach. Through his telescope, he was able to see that each was flying signals of distress. At once, he notified the station keeper, Capt. Howard Wilcox, who ordered that the station boat be manned. Immediately word was sent to the superintendent at Wakefield, and every station in the district was told to stand by to give assistance if needed. The disabled craft had also been sighted by crews of the Sandy Point station on Block Island, who made ready to assist as well. In the teeth of the gale, the hardy crew labored to launch their surf boat, but again and again they were thrown back upon the beach. The Quonochontaug crew is shown here *c.* 1910.

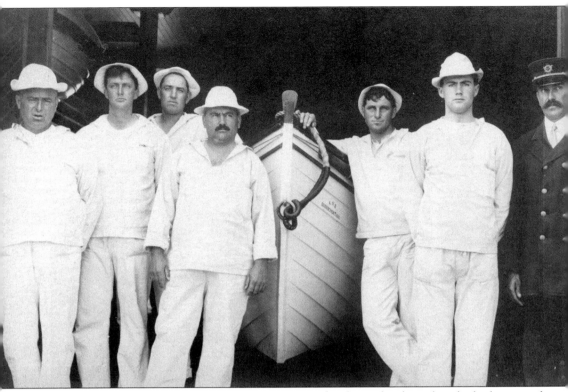

Time after time, the Quonochontaug crew attempted to leave the shore, but the high seas and terrific winds drove them back, with the water breaking in frothy masses over them. Finally, after two hours of toil, they were able to make headway, tugging their utmost at the long oars until they succeeded in getting out beyond the breakers. In the meantime, the wind had been increasing, the sea running at record heights as the lifesavers slowly made headway. As they lessened the distance to the imperiled craft, Keeper Howard Wilcox watched as a large tug hove in sight and began rescue operations. It was toward one barge in particular that the crew now directed their efforts. One of the three barges was settling rapidly with the four-man crew still on board. Fearing that the tug might not reach them in time, the lifesavers redoubled their efforts to reach the stricken craft. Progress was slow in the face of the gale, however, and the men were quickly becoming exhausted in their long labors. While still fighting foot by foot to reach the craft, a second tug was sighted heading toward the barges. Soon all three barges were taken in tow. Seeing this, Wilcox could now direct his crew to return to shore, where they stood in readiness to make another attempt if further assistance was required.

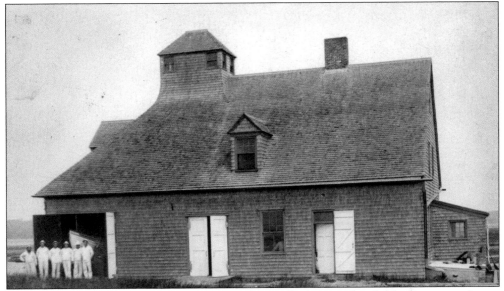

The Quonochontaug Life-Saving Station sat down Charlestown beach about seven and one-half miles east of the Watch Hill Lighthouse. What was known in the 1880s as Quonocontaug Pond was once a bustling harbor open to the ocean. Over time, heavy seas pushed sand ahead to fill up the mouth of the harbor, cutting it off from the sea. The lifesaving station, first placed here in 1892, was designed by George R. Tolman. Twenty of this style station would be built along the Atlantic coast from Massachusetts to Florida during the period from 1891 to 1908.

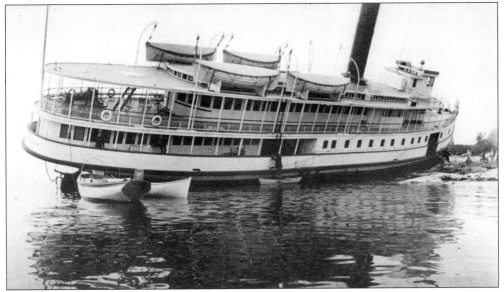

On December 20, 1883, the lookout at the Watch Hill Life-Saving Station discovered the vessel *Ellen Maria* of Bangor. It was stranded on Schooner Reef on the south side of Fisher's Island, about nine miles southwest from the station. The vessel had run ashore during a thick snowstorm and was not visible to the lifesavers until the storm cleared. The crew proceeded with all speed in their lifeboat to the vessel, but on arriving found it full of water. Shortly after arrival, the Revenue Steamer *Dexter* arrived to assist, and later wreckers were able to refloat the *Ellen Maria*.

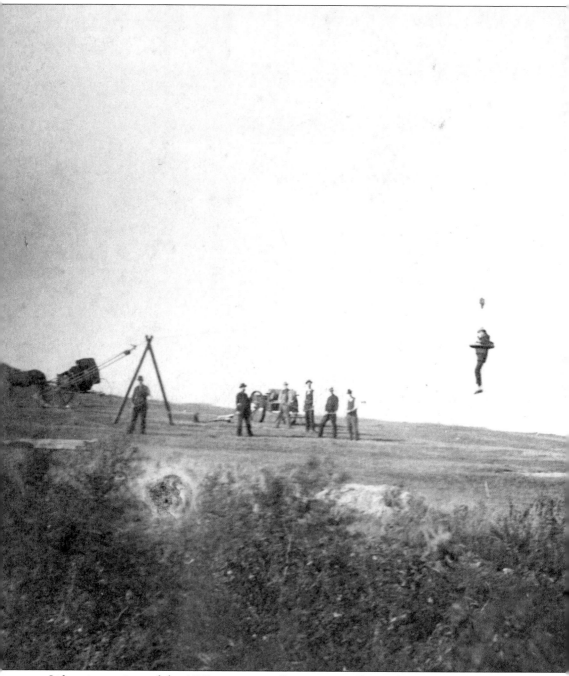

Lifesaving stations of the 1870s were typically two-story affairs. They measured 18 to 20 feet wide by 40 feet long and were painted an olive drab color. Built of tongue-and-groove pine with gable roofs, they were covered with cedar and cypress shingles and had strong shutters on the windows. On the roofs were heavy projected eaves and a small lookout deck with a flagstaff rising from it. During the early 1870s, the first major expansion of the U.S. Life-Saving Service occurred since its organization in 1848, with four stations being established in Rhode Island. The stations were all quite similar in appearance. Station keepers were required to live at or

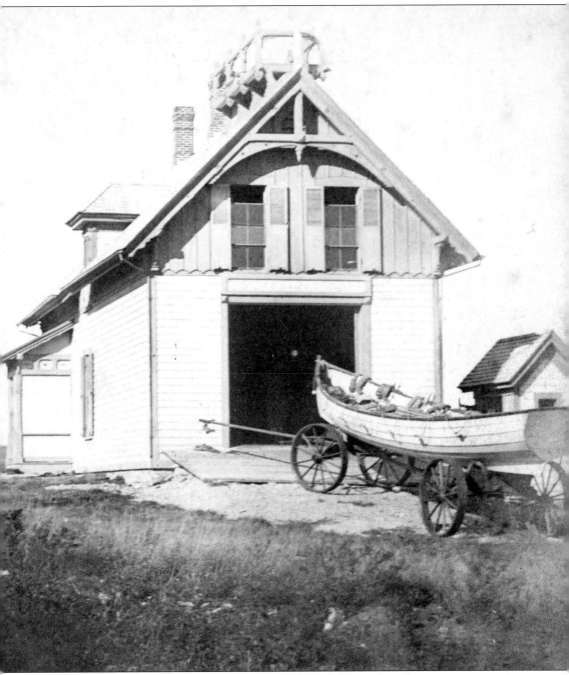

near the stations year-round, while surfmen were released during the calmer summer months from May until September. From September 1 until November 30, the stations employed six surfmen, with the addition of a seventh "winter man" from December 1 until April 30. Over its 45-year history, the U.S. Life-Saving Service would remain unsurpassed in its record of lives and property saved. The service would also lay the groundwork for what would become today's Coast Guard. Sumner Increase Kimball, general superintendent, would remain one of the most respected government administrators long after his passing in 1923 at age 89.

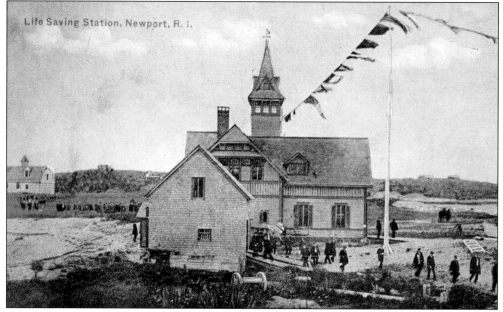

Life Saving Station, Newport, R. I.

The Brenton Point Life-Saving Station was located out on Prices Neck in Newport. Upscale communities often received fancier station designs. Newport was no exception. The station was constructed in 1884 from a design by Paul J. Pelz, who began his work with the U.S. Light-House Board designing such lighthouses as Spectacle Reef on Lake Huron. Only four stations of this design were constructed in the country.

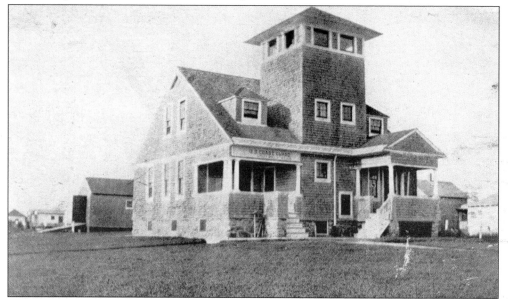

The Green Hill Life-Saving Station was located six miles west of Point Judith Lighthouse in 1911. There were only three stations of this design constructed in the country, the other two being at the Isle of Shoals, Maine, and Peaked Hill Bars, Massachusetts. Prominent in this design is the stocky square lookout tower, replacing an octagonal tower in previous designs. Crews at this station consisted of six surfman and a keeper, with an extra surfman from December through April.

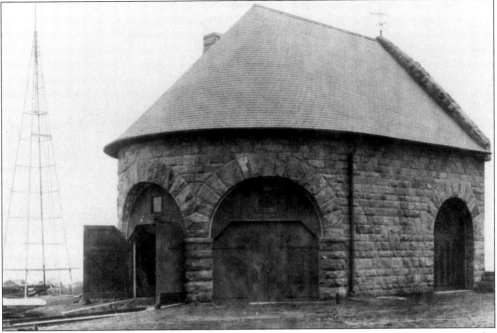

The town of Narragansett Pier boasts one of the more unusual lifesaving station designs in the entire country. The station was designed by the New York architectural firm of McKimm, Mead & White and was built in 1888. It is one of only two masonry stations constructed in the country, and its design is similar to stations once found in Great Britain. Chosen to fit in with the nearby architecture, this station survives today as a popular restaurant on Ocean Road. (Courtesy Ralph Shanks collection.)

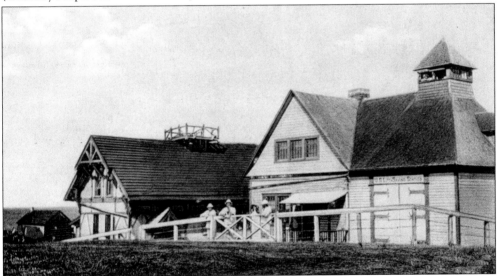

On August 26, 1767, the brig *Dolphin*, while bound from Jamaica to Newport, caught fire just off Point Judith. Although many passengers and crew members were able to make their way to shore, five women perished in their cabins. Recalling this and numerous wrecks in the area over the years, the U.S. Life-Saving Service erected the first of two stations here in 1876, seen at left in this *c.* 1900 view.

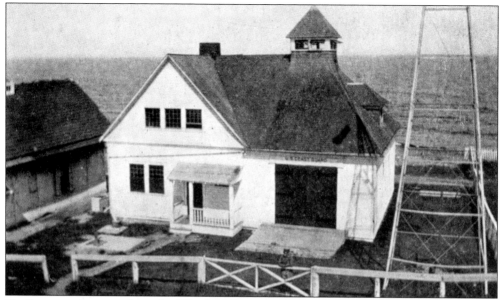

Similar somewhat in style to the Watch Hill station, this first station continued to be used for many years after its replacement was constructed at its side in 1888. This new station was similar to the New Shoreham and Block Island stations, as well as nine stations constructed over the next few years on the coast of New Jersey. This station served well into the Coast Guard era and remains in use by the Coast Guard today. It is shown in this St. Onge view from c. 1930.

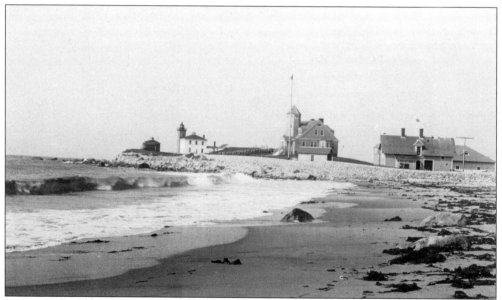

Westerly has always been a dangerous area, being partly sand and rock. Running far out into the ocean here is Watch Hill Point, which has been the scene of many dreadful disasters. The old Napatree and Sandy Points are a continuation of this promontory, enclosing a portion of the sound known as Little Narragansett Bay. The elevation of Watch Hill makes it a grand lookout point, and in 1806 a lighthouse was constructed. In 1850, one of the first two dozen lifesaving stations in the country was erected just behind the lighthouse.

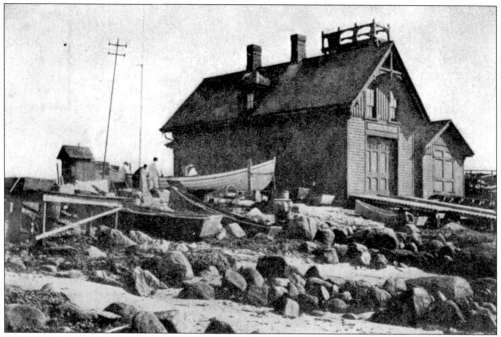

In 1879, the early lifesaving station was replaced by an 1876-type design. The station was typical of the time, with a large boat room on the first level and a smaller mess room behind, where the crews assembled and ate their meals. The second floor housed the crew's sleeping quarters with extra cots for survivors, as well as an open watchtower on the roof.

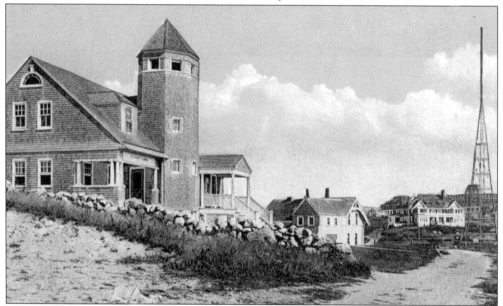

By 1907, a replacement was again needed on this exposed point, where a new building of the latest Port Huron type was constructed. Characteristic of this style is the octagonal three-story watchtower projecting from the center of the front facade. Over the years, countless wrecks occurred in this area, requiring the services of the lifesavers and (later) the Coast Guard crews that served here.

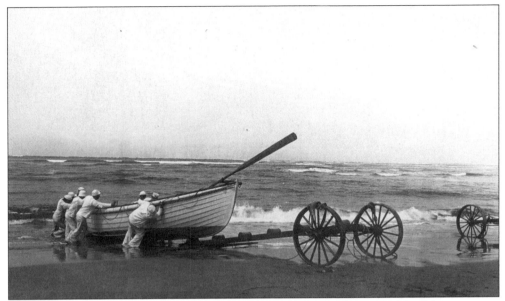

Surf boats were manned by six surfmen and the keeper. The boats used by lifesavers were designed to be smaller and lighter than the lifeboats of the day, which enabled the men to haul them the long distances down the rocky or sandy beaches to a wreck. Each surfman worked one oar while the keeper directed the operation and worked the long steering oar at the stern. Here the lifesaving crew prepares to launch a surf boat during a drill. Note the canvas bumpers to prevent damage when alongside a wreck.

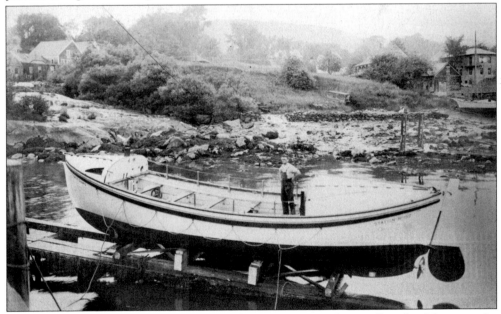

Around 1910, the U.S. Life-Saving Service began converting from pulling (oar) boats to the new motorized lifeboats. Although engines were still in their early stages of development, they afforded the lifesavers the ability to extend their range and to be less exhausted upon arrival. Thus, they would be better able to perform their rescue duties. Shown c. 1935 is a Coast Guard boat, probably a 34-foot motorized lifeboat.

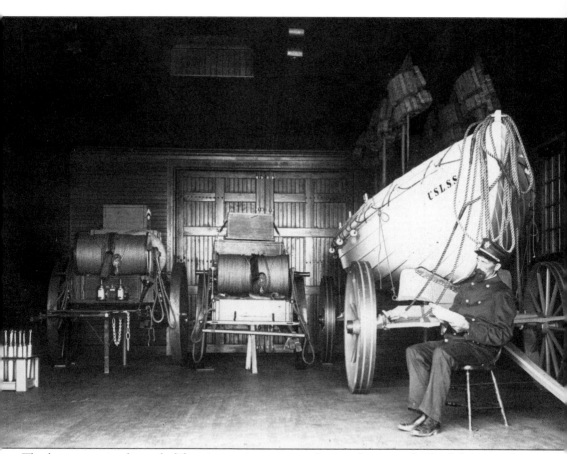

The boat room in the early lifesaving stations occupied more than two-thirds of the ground floor, opening by a broad double door to the weather. Here the boats, life car, wreck gun, and additional apparatus were stored. An 1880s station, fully equipped, cost about $5,000. These stations included all appurtenances needed and were furnished with stoves, cots, blankets, and required utensils. Stations were provided with the most approved appliances for saving people from wrecks, first among these being the six-oared surf boat. Surf boats were usually of cedar and generally from 25 to 27 feet long. Commonly, air cases were included within the ends to provide floatation, and cork fenders ran along the sides to protect against collision with wreckage. Boats generally weighed from 700 to 1,000 pounds, were rowed by six skilled surfmen, and were guided by the station keeper using a long steering oar. So great was the skill of the men in the U.S. Life-Saving Service that thousands of mariners were brought to safety in such craft. (Courtesy Vincent L. Wood collection.)

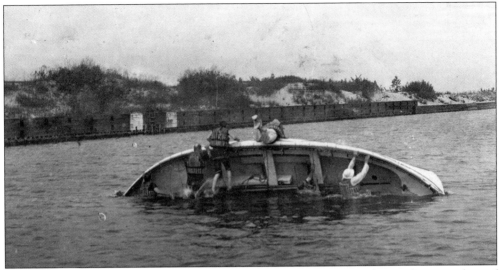

Among the drills that U.S. Life-Saving Service personnel were required to perform was the surf boat capsize drill. The ability to right a surf boat overturned by the sea was most important to the lifesaver's survival, and crews were required to become proficient at this procedure. Shanks and York, in their book *The U.S. Life-Saving Service*, note that the service record was just 13 seconds to right an overturned boat. Shown is a crew drilling in this procedure with an overturned boat.

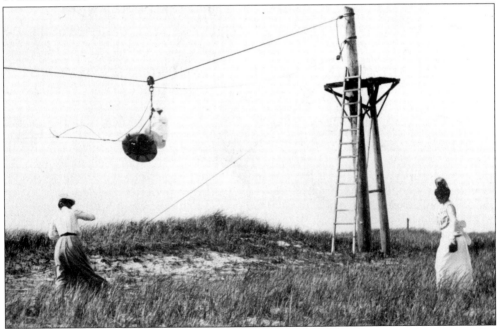

The breeches buoy apparatus was used to rescue sailors when their vessel was stranded sufficiently close to shore to be reached by a shot line from the lifesaver's Lyle gun. Drills were held daily except Sunday in this and all aspects of rescue work, flag signaling, first aid, restoration of the apparently drowned, and other requirements. These drills ensured that the men would be proficient under all conditions. Riding in the breeches buoy was a favorite pastime of Victorian summer visitors.

Five

IDA LEWIS, THE HURRICANE OF 1938, AND THE PROVIDENCE RIVER LIGHTS

Over the years, light keepers have frequently risked their lives to save shipwrecked mariners, but few have matched the record attained by Ida Lewis during her career at Lime Rock Light. Ida Zoralda Lewis was born in Newport in 1842 to Capt. Hosea Lewis, a coast pilot at the time. In 1853, Captain Lewis was appointed the first keeper at the new Lime Rock Light in Newport. By 1858, the new keeper's quarters were completed at the lighthouse and the family moved to the light. In the fall of that year, Ida rescued four people from the waters around the Lime Rock station. One evening while enjoying the summer breezes, Ida spotted four young men as their sailboat capsized. With great speed and courage, Ida immediately launched her own dory toward the victims. With constant rowing, she was finally able to reach the panicked victims, whom she pulled aboard one by one. (Manchester Brothers view, c. 1869.)

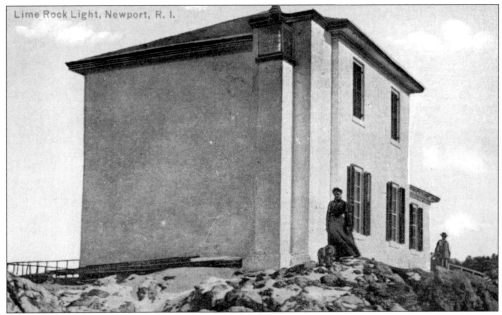

Lime Rock Light was constructed in 1854 at a cost of $1,500. It was situated on the rocks on the south side of the south entrance to Newport Harbor. The light consisted of a fixed red light from a sixth-order lantern mounted on the northwest corner of the square whitewashed dwelling. On July 18, 1927, the light at Lime Rock was deactivated and replaced by a skeleton tower. Today the site serves the Narragansett Bay Regatta Association and is known as the Ida Lewis Yacht Club.

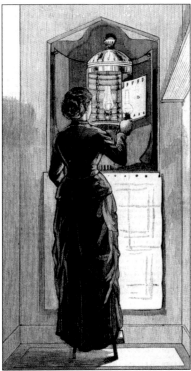

In 1872, Ida Lewis's father, Capt. Hosea Lewis, suffered a severe stroke and was unable to maintain the lighthouse. As in most lighthouse families, 16-year-old Ida was well versed in the routine of caring for the light. She often helped her father as he filled the lamp with oil and trimmed the wick, and these responsibilities later fell to Ida and her mother as unofficial keepers. In 1872, Captain Lewis passed away. By 1879, Ida was appointed as the official keeper by the U.S. Light-House Board at an annual salary of $756. (*Frank Leslie's Illustrated Newspaper*, November 5, 1881.)

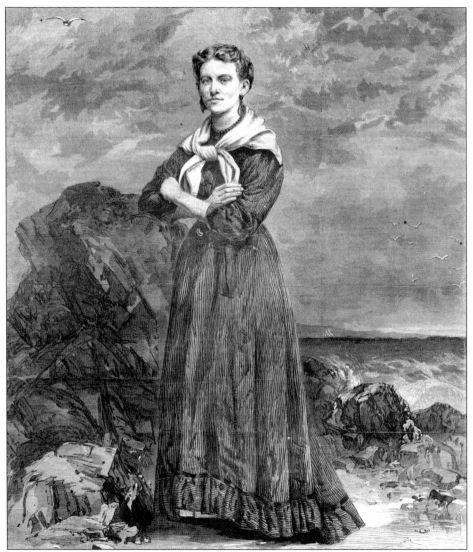

Being the oldest of the Lewis children, Ida often rowed her siblings to school and had became expert at swimming and boat handling. In the winter of 1866, Ida again showed her skill and courage when she rescued a soldier from the bay. *Harper's Weekly* reported that "it was a most daring feat, requiring courage and perseverance such as few of the male sex even are possessed of." Over the years, Ida's acts of heroism were repeated, with her most daring rescue occurring in the winter of 1869. During a frightful snowstorm, Ida looked out to see two soldiers clinging to their overturned boat. Starting out with a young boy as a guide, the soldiers were soon overtaken by the storm and were swamped. The boy was lost immediately, but the soldiers clung to their capsized craft. Although suffering from illness, Ida rushed out. With the help of her brother, she launched her dory for the men. As Ida approached, one man could hold on no longer and began to sink into the boiling sea, but Ida grabbed him by the hair and was able to maneuver him aboard. (*Harper's Weekly*, July 31, 1869.)

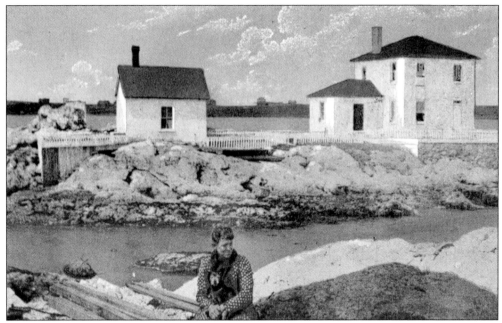

Soon Ida had the second man aboard and began the arduous row back to the lighthouse. With such a fearful gale raging, the return trip proved a perilous task, even for an experienced oarswoman like Ida. Soon, however, Ida was able to get them to the warmth and security of the lighthouse, where the two men were finally revived. This and Ida's other rescues were soon picked up by the newspapers of the day, and she became a noted heroine.

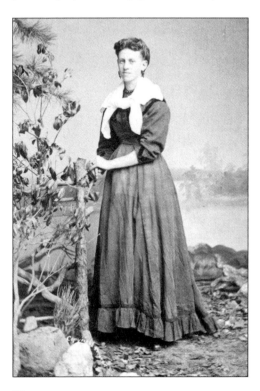

At age 28, Ida Lewis had already saved eight lives. By the end of her 54-year career, she would be credited with saving a total of 18 lives. At a time when most women were not in the professional work force, Ida Lewis overcame bias of the time to establish a record of rescues equaled by few. In 1906, at age 64, Ida Lewis performed her last rescue when she saved a woman whose boat capsized while en route to the light. (Manchester Brothers view, c. 1869.)

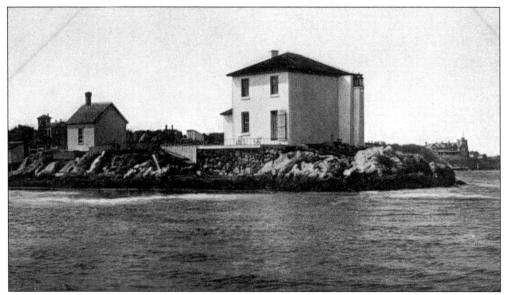

When Ida Lewis passed away in 1911, Edward Janson was transferred from Sandy Hook Light to become the new keeper. Jansen also proved to be a capable keeper when, in 1918, he was credited with saving the lives of two men whose boat had swamped during a storm. Ida's boat is now on display at the Museum of Yachting at the Fort Adams State Park. A large collection of memorabilia from Ida Lewis and her family can also be seen at the Newport Historical Society Museum.

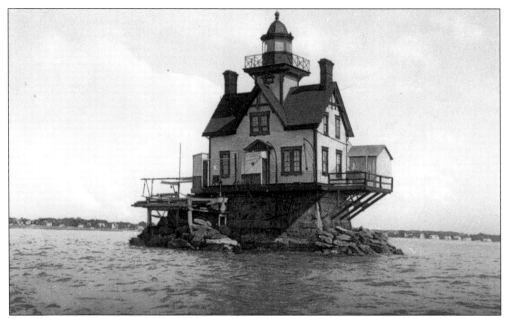

The dangerous shoal on the east side of the Providence River near Bullock Point was first marked with a portable beacon, but in 1874 this charming Victorian lighthouse was constructed. The sixth-order lantern above the front gable lends a stately appearance to the structure, as does the ironwork and ornate railings. Note the small privy extending over the right side, emptying into the water—a common practice at the time.

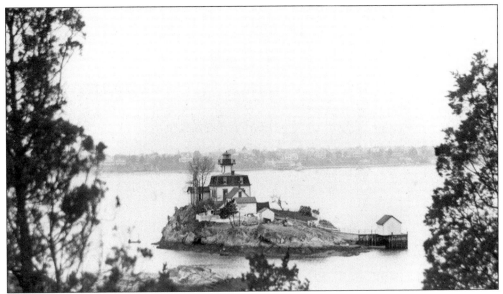

Off Pomham Rocks near the east side of the river sits Pomham Rocks Light. This attractive eight-room Victorian structure closely resembles that at Sabine Point, Rose Island, and a few other area light stations. Like most stations of the time, there was no running water here. For this, rainwater on the roof was funnelled from the gutters into brick cisterns on the ground or in the cellar.

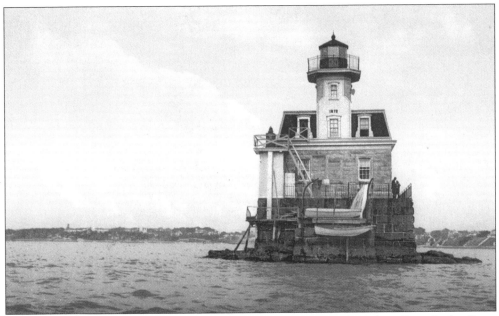

Near the easterly edge of the channel of the Providence River sat the Sabine Point Light. Since 1872, this light has marked the shoal extending southwesterly from Sabine Point. The structure was a beautiful granite dwelling with a mansard roof and a white octagonal tower rising from the front of the building. From this point at the bend in the river, the lights at Pomham, Conimicut, and Fuller Rock could easily be seen. In 1968, this lovely structure was burned to make way for a widening of the channel.

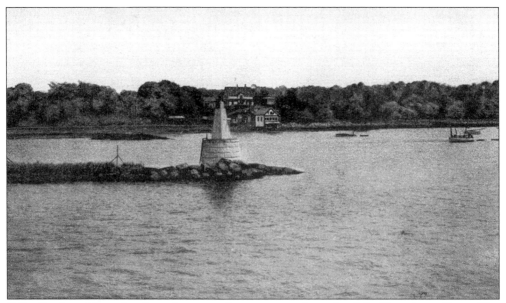

Fuller Rock and Sassafras Point lie one mile apart, on either side of the Providence River. The lights there consisted of fixed sixth-order lanterns atop a white pyramidal wooden structure. The lights were erected in 1872. Both beacons were maintained by a single keeper, who would have to battle fog and currents twice each day to row across the river. For this reason, and the low pay, keepers at this station were difficult to retain.

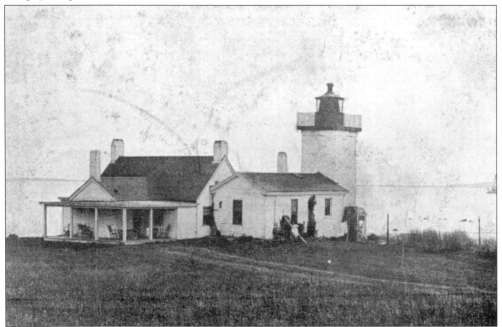

Nayatt Point Light in Barrington consisted of a 23-foot-tall brick tower equipped with six oil lamps, each with a nine-inch reflector. The light tower was attached to a small, one-and-a-half-story keeper's dwelling with a small kitchen and porch. Today, this structure, located on Nayatt Point Road, is a private dwelling. Views from here are most pleasing and include a clear view of the 1882 Conimicut Light.

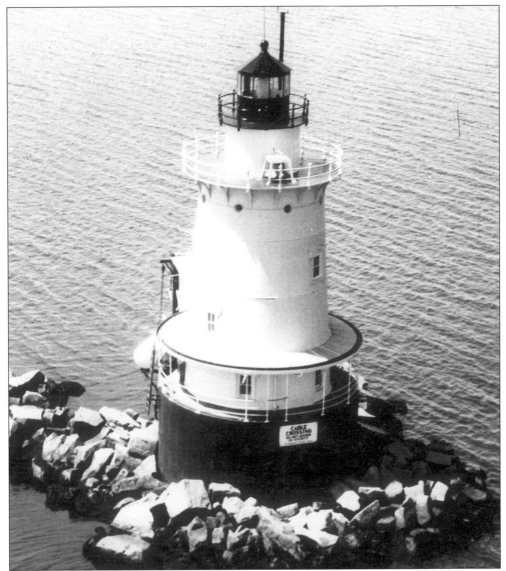

The first lighthouse at Conimicut Point was lit in 1868, displaying a fourth-order flashing white light. However, since there was no dwelling located at the light, Keeper Davis Perry and his assistants were required to row the one mile to and from the light each day, regardless of the weather. In 1873, a roomy dwelling was constructed for the keepers on the pier supporting the light. However, during a particularly severe winter in 1875, the keepers were forced to withdraw as ice floes worked against the dwelling, destroying it and the keeper's belongings. The stone light tower was demolished in 1882, and soon this conical cast-iron tower on a brown cylindrical base would take its place. The lantern cast a fixed white light in the fourth order with a red sector delineating the shoals. It was visible for 13 miles. On the lower lantern gallery was a fog bell, which was struck by a weight-driven machine during periods of fog. Most keepers enjoyed the isolation of this outpost, and the station continued to be manned until the 1960s, when it was automated. The light remains today and can be seen from Nayatt Point or by boat. This Coast Guard photograph was taken c. the 1940s. (Author's collection.)

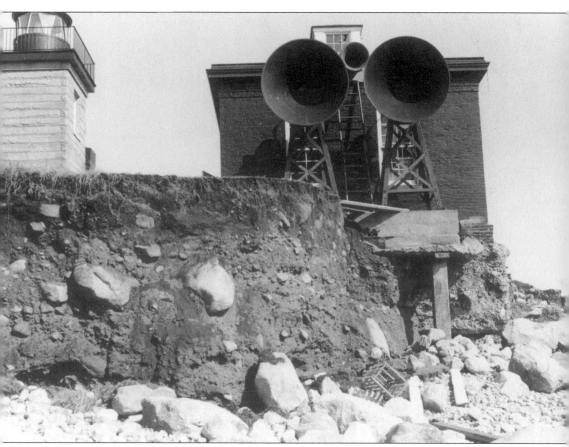

The forecast for New England was reassuring on that hot Wednesday in September 1938, and residents of coastal areas saw no reason for concern. Of more importance that week was the more than 10 inches of rain that had fallen in the previous five days. Some areas in Massachusetts had been evacuated as the earth became saturated and rivers began to swell. No news of the onrushing fury of this new storm was received until September 21, when it struck the coast of New Jersey. The storm had traveled over 600 miles in 12 hours, one of the fastest movements ever recorded. As the rain persisted, rivers overflowed their banks, compounding an unusually high tide. As the storm drove up the Connecticut Valley late that afternoon, huge wind-driven waves of saltwater slammed into the coastal towns. Residents began to take shelter wherever they could. While waves were pushed ahead by the gale, communities along the entire coast shivered and waited. The men of the Coast Guard worked to keep the lights shining to guide mariners in distress and to effect rescues where possible. This photograph shows the damage to Beavertail Lighthouse. (Courtesy Coast Guard Historian's Office.)

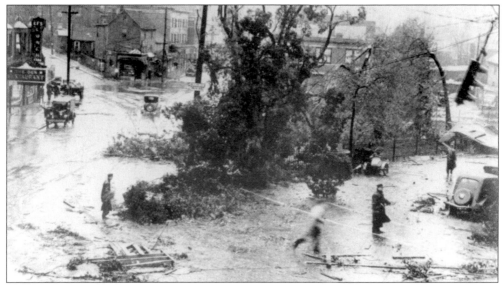

Although western Connecticut suffered severely, its losses paled in comparison to those of the regions east of Saybrook and north of Norwich. In New London, the anemometer was reading a 98 mph wind speed when it was blown away as the hurricane struck. Four hours later, when the wind began to slacken, whole sections of the city lay in ruins. Barges, the lighthouse tender *Tulip*, yachts, and hundreds of small craft crashed against buildings or were tossed into the streets, blocking traffic.

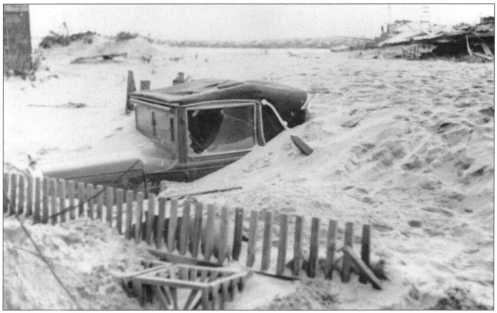

At Westerly and Watch Hill, the sea claimed entire settlements. On Prudence Island, the water ate away the banking up to the iron lighthouse while six residents of the island perished. Despite the light keeper's best efforts, his wife and son were carried away by the seas as their house was swept into the sea. The keeper only narrowly escaped the same fate by securing himself within the iron lighthouse tower. Shown here is Point Judith. (Courtesy Coast Guard Historian's Office.)

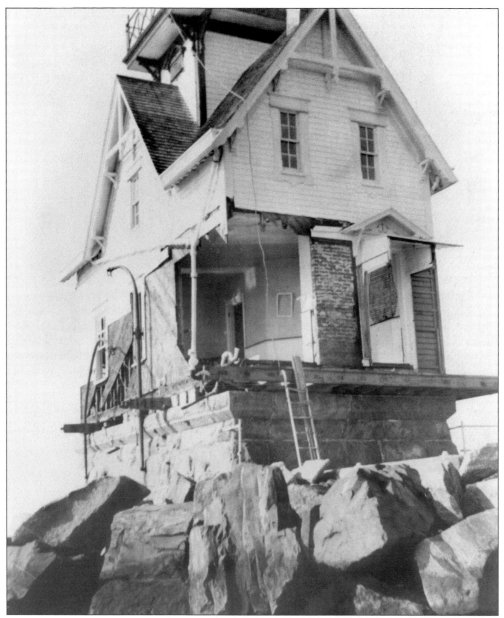

Grim scenes repeated themselves throughout the region as the hurricane approached. Keeper Andrew Zuius Sr. at Bullock Point redoubled his efforts to keep the light shining. Although mountainous seas tore away the end wall from the structure, Zuius climbed to the second floor and kept the burner in operation. As the boiling green seas built up against the light, the granite foundation under the dwelling became undermined and began to crumble. Soon the end walls were breached by the sea and, when the storm subsided, Zuius found that all of his supplies, his belongings, and the station boat had been washed away. At Whale Rock Light, the cast-iron light tower had stood since 1882, its iron V-base bolted to the subsurface rock. Before the night was over, this too would be thrown into the raging sea with its keeper alone in the tower. Near Westhampton, where 50 cottages were swept into the sea, the Coast Guard found 11 adults and one child huddling behind a sand dune for protection. (Courtesy Coast Guard Historian's Office.)

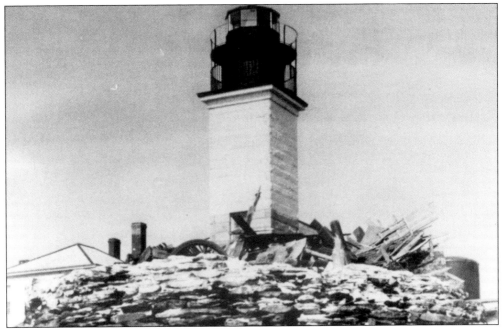

While onlookers helplessly watched the devastation, Prudence Island and the lighthouses at Beavertail, Bullock's Point, and Whale Rock were enduring similar onslaughts by the storm. In Jamestown at Beavertail Lighthouse, the fog whistle house was torn away, revealing an earlier foundation. This foundation was probably that of the original wood lighthouse that occupied the site in 1749. (Coast Guard photograph; author's collection.)

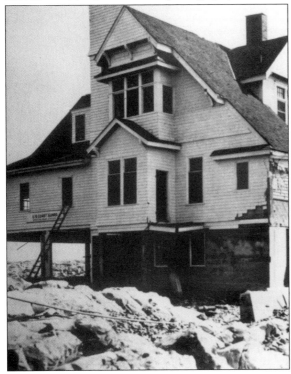

At Brenton Point off Newport, the Coast Guard station was ripped by the winds and pounded by the sea. Much of the bottom level of the building was torn away as the men fought to save their station. The next morning, as the storm proceeded northward, the waters began to recede almost as fast as they had risen. By 10 A.M., residents began to venture out to view the devastation and to count the dead. In all, more than 682 men, women, and children perished. Thousands were injured. (Coast Guard photograph; author's collection.)

Six

THE LIGHTSHIPS

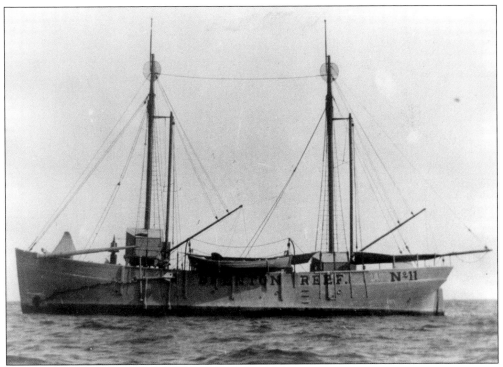

Lightships were used to mark offshore shoals in places where a lighthouse could not be constructed. Such vessels came into use in the United States in 1819. Between 1820 and 1983, 116 lightship stations were established around the country. Because of the treacherous nature of the New England coastline, the coast from Portland, Maine, to Stratford Shoal in Connecticut boasted more light vessels than any other similar stretch in the country. Brenton Reef (named for a prominent Newport family) lies at the extreme southern point of Rhode Island, about three and a half miles west of Beavertail Lighthouse, and marks the approaches into Narragansett Bay. Light Vessel No. 14 was first placed on station in 1853 and served until 1856, when it was replaced by LV-11, a wood-hulled, two-masted vessel. On the top of the mastheads, the round netlike objects are day recognition signals, or daymarks, making them visible from a distance. Two sets of oil lamps with reflectors, one set on each mast of the vessel, were visible for 11 miles. Also included was a hand-rung fog bell. Later, a horn was added to serve as a fog signal. During its first year, LV-11 was blown onto the rocks off Brenton Reef in a gale causing severe damage to the frame and rudder. The vessel was soon repaired, however, and returned to its station. On November 26, 1890, it was again damaged when struck by the SS *Curlew*, a British ship. (National Archives photograph; courtesy Nautical Research Centre.)

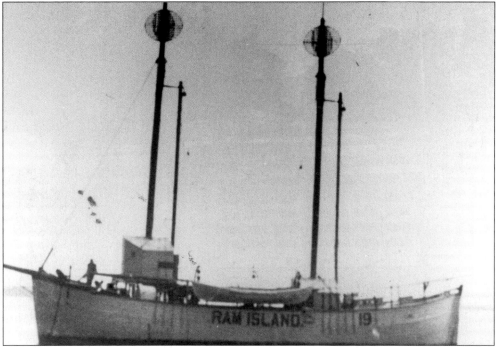

The Ram Island Ledge light vessel was moored in 42 feet of water off Ram Island Reef in Fishers Island Sound. The area is located south of the town of Mystic, about two miles from the Lattimer Reef Lighthouse. The light vessel here served as a guide for vessels approaching the ports of Mystic and Noank. LV-19 served on this station from 1886 until 1894, when replaced by LV-23. (National Archives photograph; courtesy Shore Village Museum.)

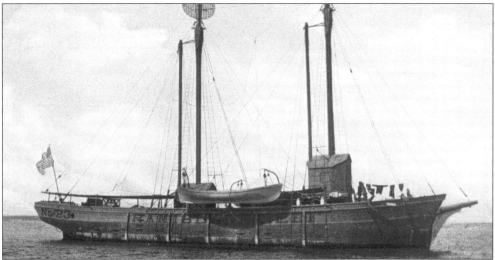

LV-23 served on Ram Island Ledge from 1894 until 1925, when the station was discontinued. Having been a schooner at one time, LV-23 was converted to a light vessel in 1862. The vessel was constructed of oak and yellow pine and measured 94 feet in length. In February 1904, the master was ordered to remove the vessel from station for four days, an unusual occurrence. The ice was extremely heavy and it was feared that the vessel would be damaged or lost. This *c.* 1906 view was taken by the Robbins Brothers Company.

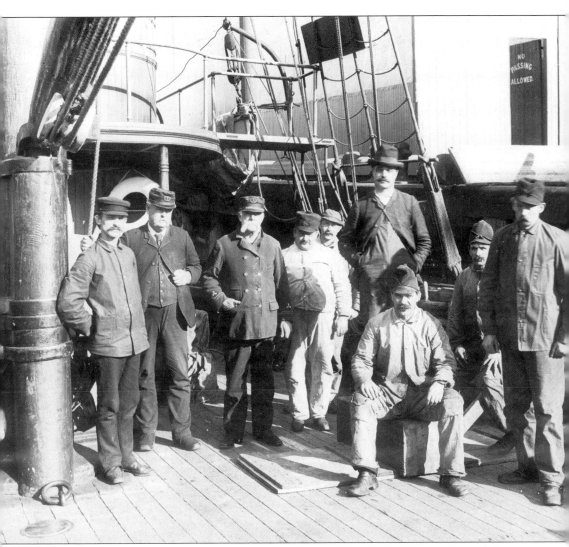

Storms, the ravages of the sea, loneliness, and cold took their toll on sailors who manned these early light vessels. Life on board a New England lightship was anything but placid. Although an occasional warm summer afternoon could be a relief, the unpredictable ocean and New England storms caused great hardships among the crews. Early lightships were cold and damp, and they had only the sparest of comforts, as most of the space was allocated to fuel and stores. Robert Thayer Sterling noted in his book *Lighthouses of the Maine Coast*: "Lightship was a terrible roller. During a storm she would shiver and shake when the big seas struck." At times, lightships pitched and rolled such that even experienced whalemen felt squeamish. Life aboard for months on end could be described as a term of solitary confinement, combined with the horrors of seasickness. So vehement was the pitching and rolling that the pots and kettles were lashed to the stove to prevent them from taking flight. In the winter, the ice might extend for 12 feet or more on each side of the bow, with a thick layer covering the vessel's deck and gear.

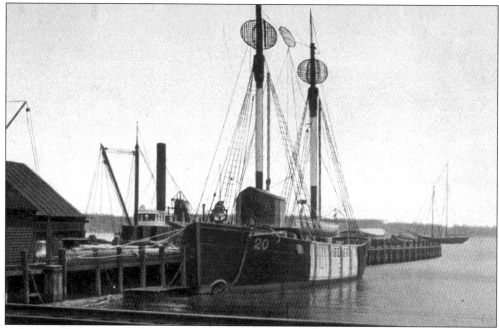

Light Vessel No. 20 served as a relief vessel in Connecticut waters from 1886 until 1918. The vessel was involved in a collision in 1888 and was rammed in 1894 by three sailing vessels, stoving in her boats and twisting her stem. In 1900, the vessel was damaged in a collision, as were many light vessels when on station. In 1918, the mainmast was removed and replaced with a single acetylene lens lantern. This photograph, taken prior to 1918, shows Light Vessel No. 20 at the lighthouse depot in New London.

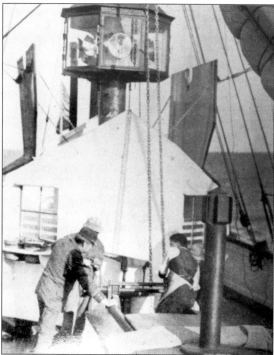

A typical light vessel of the 1870s was a schooner of 275 tons, 103 feet long overall. Its fore and aft lantern masts were 71 feet high, and directly behind each was a mast for sails. Forty-four feet up the lantern masts were daymarks, reddish-brown hoop-iron gratings that would enable other vessels to sight the lightship during the day more readily. The lanterns were octagons of glass in copper frames, five feet in diameter, encircling the mast. Within the lanterns were eight oil lamps with parabolic reflectors.

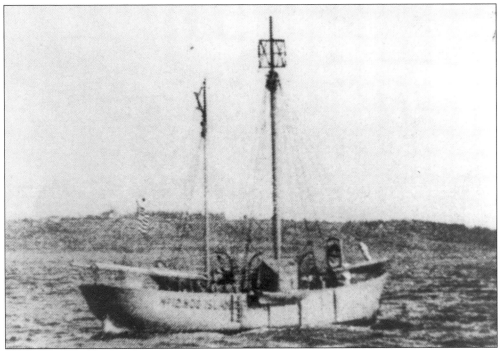

Hog Island Shoal Light Vessel No. 12 was located at the junction of Narragansett Bay and Mount Hope Bay. This location served as a mark for ship traffic bound north for Providence, and for eastbound traffic to Bristol and Fall River. The Lighthouse Service maintained LV-12 on this station from 1885 to 1901, when the Hog Island Shoal Lighthouse was established. (Courtesy Nautical Research Centre.)

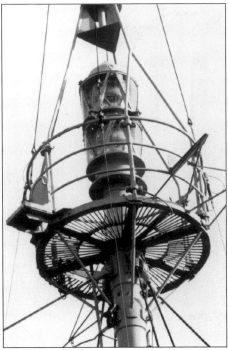

Light vessel lamps were raised to the main masthead at dusk and consisted of a single lantern with up to eight oil burners with reflectors within. By the 1890s, oil lens lanterns would be in use, clustered three or four about each masthead. Soon acetylene would come into use and many lamps were converted to burn the cleaner fuel. By 1900, however, electricity had been tamed and most lanterns utilized this new form of energy. The electric duplex lens lantern shown here dates from c. 1940. (Courtesy Shore Village Museum.)

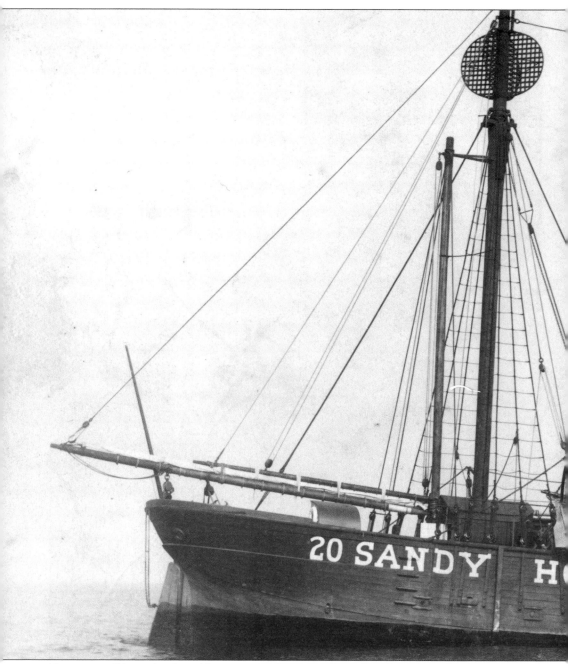

Numerous offshore shoals and bars presented a serious hazard to shipping. Often, a caisson and lighthouse would be constructed where the waters were shallow. However, where shoals continually shifted or where no fixed structure could be placed, light vessels would be used. Lightships could be easily moored near shifting shoals or bars and could be moved when the shifting sands demanded. These vessels, moored in deep waters, served also as a landfall for transoceanic shipping traffic. However, being located in these exposed positions placed them at high risk from collisions and severe storms. Conditions on these early vessels were close to uninhabitable, as the crews were forced to endure rolling and violent pitching and severe

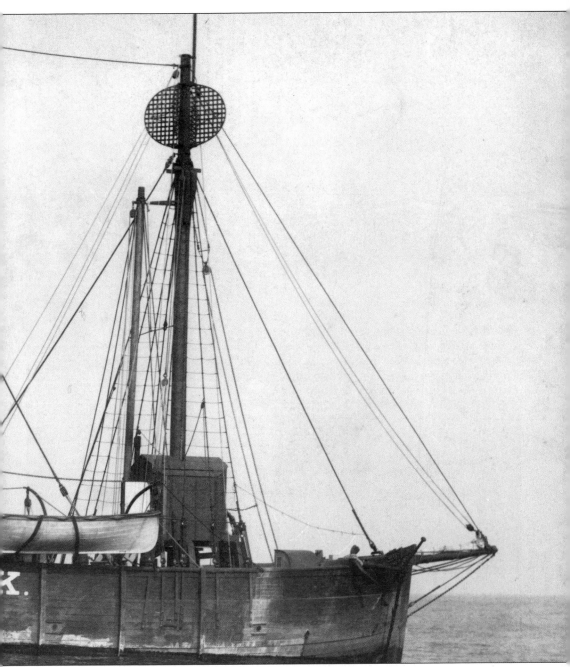

storms, resulting in frequent loss of anchors and damage to the vessels. Ultimately, designs would improve, but the service was not without serious losses. Records of the U.S. Lighthouse Service contain 237 instances of lightships being blown adrift or dragged off station in severe weather or moving ice. In addition, monotony and the danger of collision were always present. Some 150 collisions were logged, with five light vessels lost and many more damaged. Less than a dozen light vessels remain today, a few preserved as museums, a testimony to the courage and perseverance of their crews. Shown c. 1890 is Light Vessel No. 20, which served as a relief in Connecticut waters from 1886 to 1918.

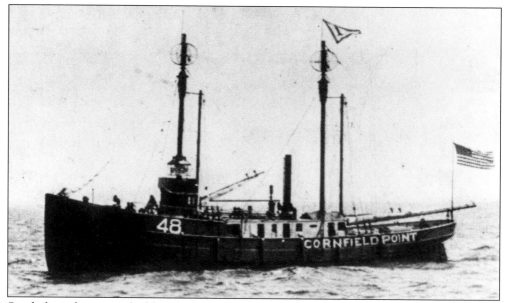

South from the town of Old Saybrook, at the mouth of the Connecticut River, lies Cornfield Point. The Cornfield Point Station was established here as a reference for vessels passing through Long Island Sound. LV-48 served on this station for 30 years, beginning in 1895. Note the steam fog whistle just forward of the smokestack and the triangular flag flying from the mast. This flag, with a red lighthouse on a white background, was the ensign of the U.S. Lighthouse Service. (Courtesy Shore Village Museum.)

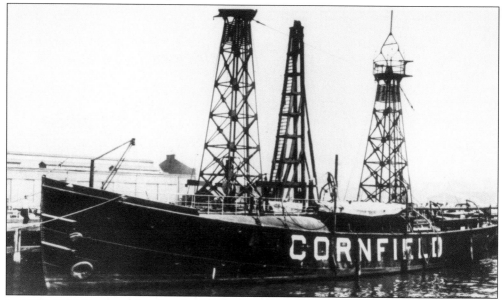

In 1926, LV-44 took up the Cornfield Point Station and served there for the next 13 years. It was the last lightship in the U.S. Lighthouse Service to be provided with no sails or propelling machinery. The vessel was also distinctive because it had two skeleton towers rather than the traditional masts, supporting an occulting electric light that was visible for 12 miles. During the Hurricane of 1938, LV-44 was badly damaged and was subsequently retired from duty. (Courtesy Shore Village Museum.)

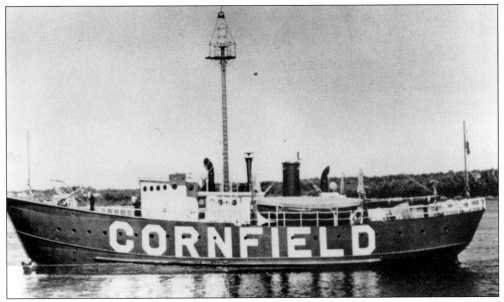

In 1939, LV-118 was commissioned and placed at the Cornfield Point Station. The vessel was diesel propelled and steel hulled, with a duplex electric lens lantern. It was the last lightship built by the U.S. Lighthouse Service and featured numerous safety features, including watertight compartments. In 1957, it was transferred off this station and, in 1972, was sold to the Lewes, Delaware Historical Society. Marked "Overfalls" (although it never served there), the vessel remains on display today. (Coast Guard photograph; courtesy Shore Village Museum.)

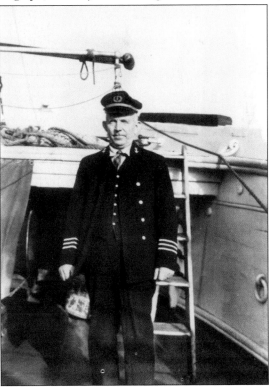

Light vessels carried a crew of 6 to 17 men and never moved from their station unless hurricanes or ice dragged them off. Duty on board New England's light vessels was rugged at best, and life was rarely dull. When storm warnings were flown along the coast and shipping headed for port, New England light vessels secured loose gear and settled down to ride the storm out. Shown is Theodore Anderson, who served as mate from 1923 to 1927 and as master from 1927 to 1935. (Courtesy Shore Village Museum.)

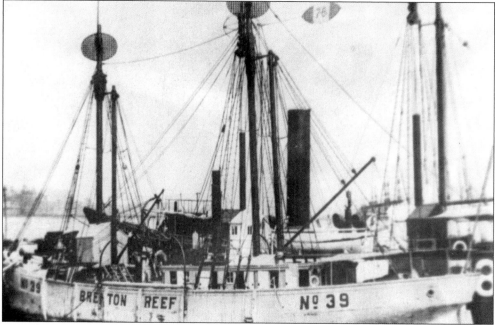

In 1897, LV-39 took up Brenton Reef Station, serving there until 1935. Until 1921, oil was still the chief illuminant, but from then until her retirement, acetylene burners were used in place of the dirtier burning oil. In August 1905, the lightship was struck by the battleship USS *Iowa*, carrying away part of the stem and damaging the headstays.

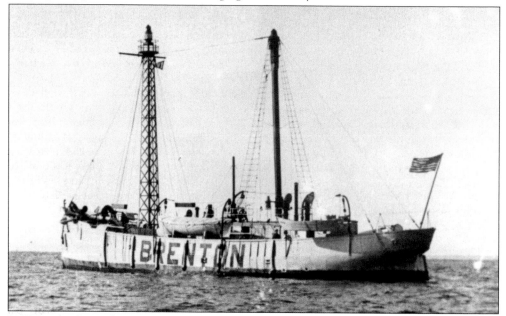

In 1921, the forward mast on LV-39 was converted to a skeleton tower and fitted out with the latest acetylene lighting apparatus. The occulting light was now visible for 12 miles from its 57-foot-high perch. The triangular U.S. Lighthouse Service flag can just be seen flying from the forward mast. Note also the ship's lifeboat for use in an emergency. (Coast Guard photograph; courtesy Shore Village Museum.)

90

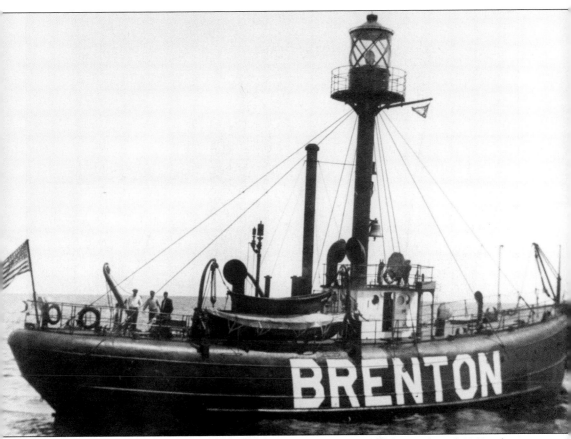

Light Vessel No. 102 was assigned to Brenton Reef Station in 1935 and served until 1962, when it was transferred to the Cross Rip Station in Massachusetts. The vessel was originally constructed for the Southwest Pass Station in Louisiana and was of a new steel "whaleback hull" design, intended to increase stability. Due to its extremely short length and draft, however, the vessel's seaworthiness was somewhat limited, and its use was confined to the more protected inside stations. The vessel, which cost $125,000 when it was constructed in 1913, was self propelled and displayed a large tubular-style lantern on a central mast. Illuminating apparatus consisted of a 500-millimeter, fifth-order lens with six flash panels and a kerosene lamp that revolved by a weight-driven clockwork mechanism. In 1917, the lamp was changed to incandescent oil vapor and was electrified in 1932. After being transferred and serving on Cross Rip until 1963, Light Vessel No. 102 was sold and worked fishing out of Ketchican, Alaska. (Coast Guard photograph; courtesy Shore Village Museum.)

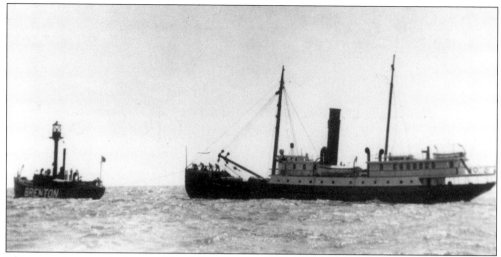

This rare photograph shows a Third District tender, possibly the *Tulip*, servicing the Brenton Reef Light Vessel No. 102 in the 1930s. Light vessels rarely left their stations, requiring the tenders to periodically deliver fuel and supplies. When weather permitted and the tender was able to bring out a relief crew, the lightship crews would be rotated ashore. During the early years, crew members averaged eight months at sea and four months ashore. (Coast Guard photograph; courtesy Shore Village Museum.)

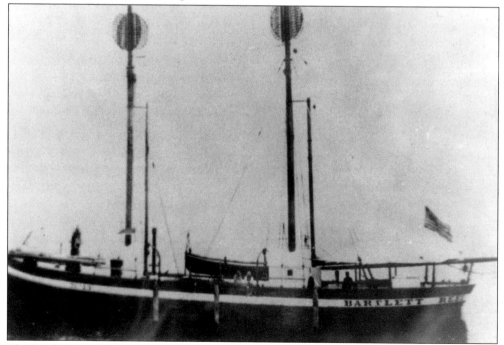

The Bartlett Reef light vessel was located three and a half miles southwest of the New London lighthouse, marking the reefs lying in the approaches to New London. The station here was in service from 1835 until 1933. Vessels serving on the Bartlett Reef Station were carried off station by ice on four occasions. In 1888, Light Vessel No. 13 was struck by a coal barge. Shown here, LV-13 served on this station from 1867 until 1933, when the station was discontinued. (National Archives photograph; courtesy Nautical Research Centre.)

Seven

CONNECTICUT LIGHTS

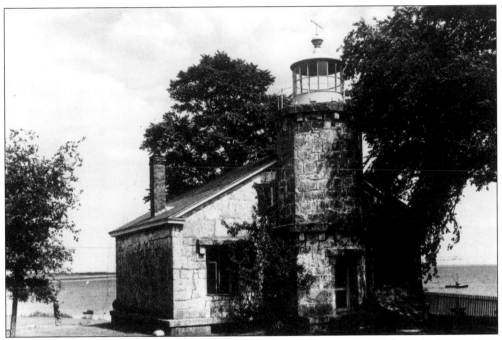

Although Connecticut is the nation's third smallest state, it remains as rich as any in maritime history. Its coastal region long played a role in the development of the nation and its maritime trade. The countryside in the region boasts rolling hills, thick forests, rushing brooks, and rivers traveling toward the rocky and sandy shore. From Stonington in the north to Stamford in the south, the Connecticut coastline provides a fascinating trip into our maritime past. Stonington has always been associated with the sea, bounded on three sides by water, as has Mystic, though not a town at all. The Mystic area is really a part of two towns—Groton, to the west of the river, and Stonington, to the east. Groton and Noank, originally a part of New London, turned their attention to the sea early on, as they border the Thames River, the New London River, and Long Island Sound. From New London, with its excellent deep harbor, to Lyme, Old Saybrook, and southward to Norwalk and Stamford, the area has long been intertwined with maritime life. Stonington Harbor Light was first constructed in 1823, but a new structure was necessary by 1840. At that time, a charming granite tower and attached keeper's quarters was constructed farther inland. Even the stairway in this six-room cottage was constructed of granite. In 1856, a sixth-order lens (the service's smallest) was installed. It was used until the light was discontinued in 1889.

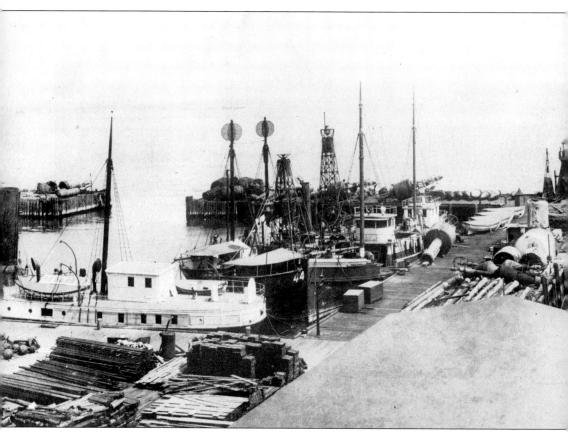

At the beginning of the 20th century, the Third District had six lighthouse tenders in service—the *John Rodgers*, *Cactus*, *Gardenia*, *Larkspur*, *Iris*, and *Mistletoe*. A typical tender of the era was a steel side-wheeled screw steamer, coal-burning with a walking beam engine. Tenders were used to deliver fuel and supplies to lighthouses and light vessels within the district and to repair buoys and navigational aids. As an example, in 1901, the *Gardenia* visited more than 200 light stations. The crew repaired 559 buoys, delivered 593 tons of coal, numerous loads of rations and supplies, and steamed thousands of miles. Another duty of the tender was to transport the district lighthouse inspector to each station for a periodic inspection. When the inspector was aboard, the tender would fly the inspector's white triangular pennant, which would alert the keeper that the inspector was on board. Keepers and families would always watch for this pennant, for it meant that all must be in order and polished to perfection. Shown in this *c.* 1910 image is the lighthouse depot at Tompkinsville, New York. At the docks are two tenders and three light vessels, including LV-44 while serving on Northeast End, New Jersey.

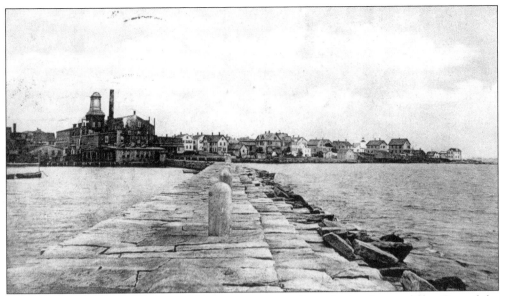

This 1906 view shows the town of Stonington as seen from the breakwater light. One of the busiest ports on the coast during the age of sail, Stonington was the site of a bustling shipbuilding industry for more than 200 years. If you look toward Stonington Point near the right, you can make out the 1840 light tower of the Stonington Harbor Light.

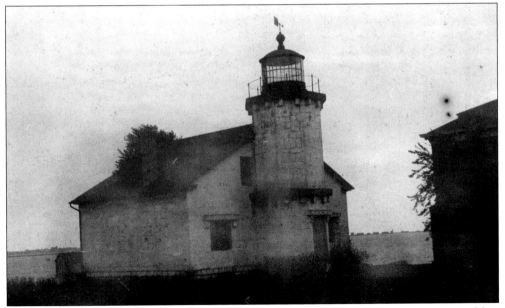

The Stonington Harbor Light has always been an important part of the community and has been lovingly preserved since 1908. At that time, a separate dwelling for the keeper of the breakwater light was constructed and the lighthouse was then purchased by the local historical society. Today this structure remains a historical museum. Maintained by society members to preserve the area's maritime history, the light provides a wonderful day trip destination.

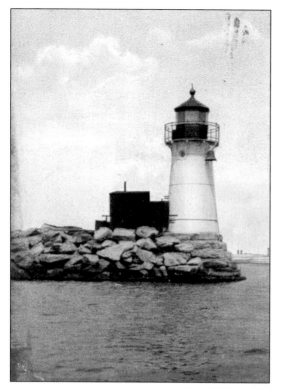

At the east end of the inner, or west, breakwater in Stonington Harbor sat the 25-foot conical iron tower of Stonington Breakwater Light. The white painted structure was built in 1889 on an octagonal granite foundation, forming the end of the breakwater. From its fourth-order iron lantern, a fixed red beam visible for 11 miles served to mark the harbor entrance.

The three-story lighthouse on New London (Southwest) Ledge represents the best in lighthouse design and construction. Probably more recognizable on a city's residential neighborhood, the stately French Second Empire building with a mansard roof seems quite at home marking New London's sharp ledge and shoal in its east entrance. The building's many white-trimmed windows and dormers accent this wonderful example of U.S. Lighthouse Service design.

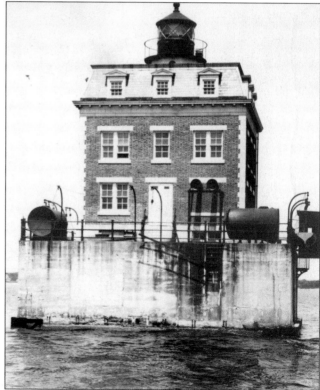

Atop the three-story, 11-room brick structure sat the fourth-order lantern that housed the light's Fresnel lens from 1909 to 1984. These lenses floated on a bed of mercury and were rotated by a weight-driven clockwork mechanism, identical to the Gamewell apparatus used at many New England fire stations for sounding their steam fire alerting whistles. Today this light is still an active aid to navigation, having been automated in 1986.

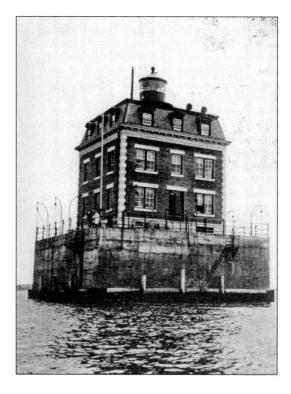

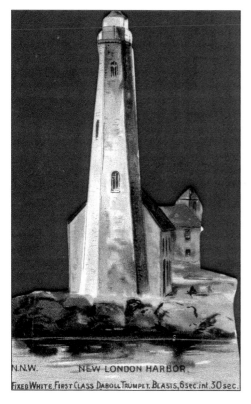

N.N.W.   NEW LONDON HARBOR.
Fixed White, First Class Daboll Trumpet, Blasts, 6 sec. int. 30 sec.

On cold nights, the lamps required constant attention to trim the wicks and keep the oil warm to prevent congealing. In addition, snow and salt spray that had built up on the lantern panes required the keeper to wash and scrape the lantern glass to keep it clear. In time, the multiple lamps were replaced by a single kerosene or incandescent oil vapor lamp, the single flame of which would be magnified a thousandfold by the rotating Fresnel prisms surrounding the lamp.

97

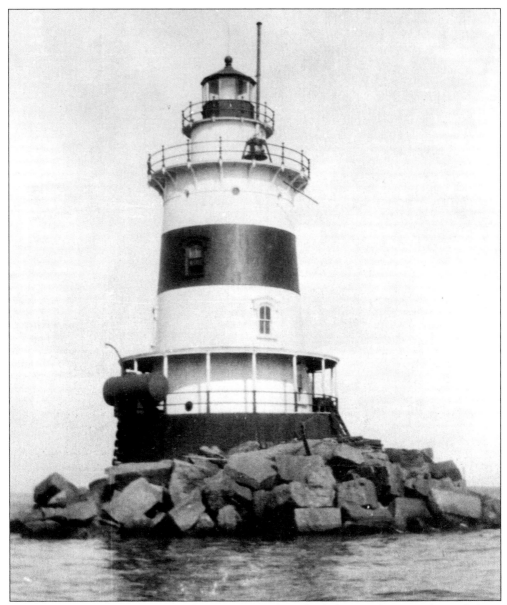

Latimer Reef Light was constructed in 1884 to replace the light vessel stationed at Eel Grass Shoal near the entrance to Stonington Harbor. As early as 1804, the reef was marked with an iron daymark, but a lighthouse became necessary by the 1880s. The cast-iron tower was marked in the 1890s with a distinctive brown band midway up the tower to distinguish it from similar lights in the area. The interior living quarters consisted of three levels, with the fourth serving as a watch room for the keeper on duty. The floors were hardwood over iron plates, and the curved walls were fitted with arched niches to serve as storage. Such cast-iron lights became common in the Northeast during the late 1800s. It was found that this design stood well against the severe Northeast winters and could be used on reefs, bars, and even atop breakwaters. As costs became more important, such standardized designs proved less costly and allowed the U.S. Lighthouse Service to reuse existing plans and parts. Today the light remains in operation, having been automated in 1974.

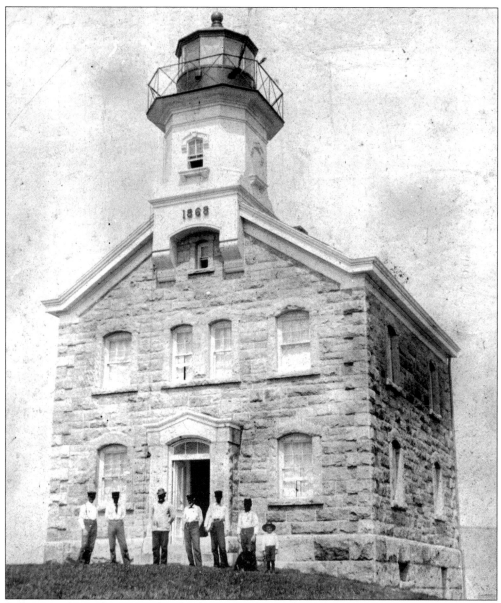

Sailing north up the west side of Fishers Island Sound near Noank, you come upon Morgan Point Light, marking the mouth of the channel of the Mystic River. The first lighthouse here was built in 1831 on the southern tip of the point. It consisted of a white granite tower and a remote keeper's dwelling. The first lights consisted of 10 whale oil lamps with parabolic reflectors. By 1850, however, a cleaner-burning single lamp was installed, making the work of the keeper in trimming wicks much less tedious. By 1867, a new building was needed and today's granite structure was constructed. As can be seen from its 133-year history, the new lighthouse was of the finest design and construction. The design chosen for this location could also be seen on Block Island, Old Field Point (New York), and Great Captain Island in Greenwich. The granite walls were constructed extremely thick (almost two feet), and all have slate roofs. All of these lights have survived the many hurricanes and storms over the years to still exhibit their charm to visitors to the area.

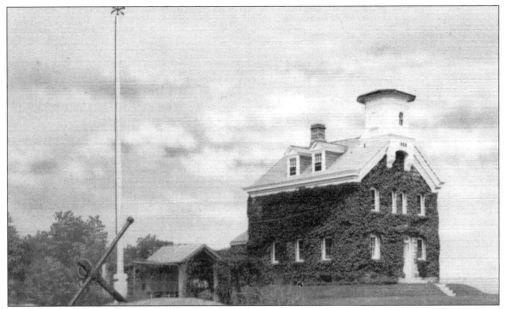

As shipping in the area began to decline, the need for a manned lighthouse on Morgan Point became somewhat less. In 1922, the light was decommissioned, to be replaced by an automatic iron beacon at the channel entrance. Today the lighthouse is wonderfully maintained in private hands. Still visible too are the remains of the oil house. Author Harlan Hamilton notes that in dry weather, you can still see the outline of the circular 1831 tower.

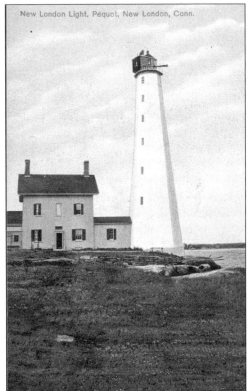

The first New London Harbor Lighthouse was built in 1760 on the west side of the entrance to New London Harbor to mark the entrance to the Thames River. The light was situated on a rocky point westward of the entrance to the Thames, and two miles from the town of New London. The lighthouse, built of stone, was 64 feet tall and 24 feet around the base.

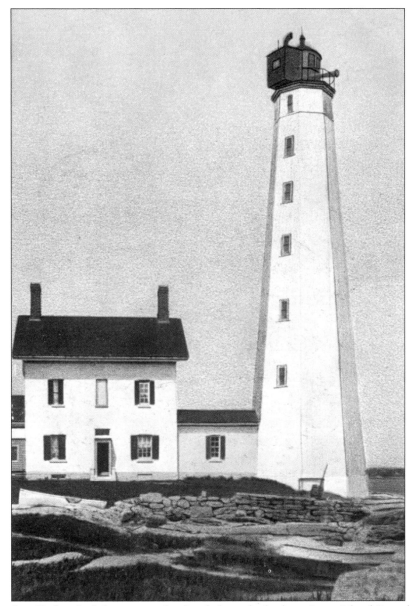

New London Harbor Lighthouse was the first light to be built on Long Island Sound and was the fourth or fifth oldest lighthouse in the United States. It was also among the original 12 Colonial lights that the federal government acquired from the states in 1789. The light was paid for by taxes levied on shipping and use of the harbor, with George Washington himself signing the contract to purchase oil for this lighthouse. By 1799, the tower had fractured, with a 10-foot crack running from the top down the side of the lighthouse. The government decided to build a new lighthouse here because, in addition to the crack, they had also received complaints that the lighthouse was not visible to vessels entering the harbor from the west. On May 7, 1800, Congress appropriated $15,700 for rebuilding the light. The new tower was completed in 1801—a substantial, 89-foot-tall building of freestone that was smooth hammered and laid in courses. The light tower was octagonal in shape. The tower tapered at the top and was ascended by an interior stairway of wood.

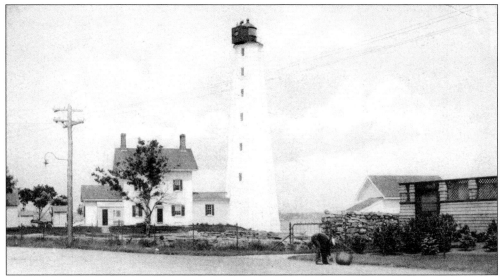

The lighting apparatus consisted of 11 lamps with parabolic reflectors, dispersed around two horizontal tables with reflectors 13 inches in diameter. In 1855, a fourth-order lens was recommended and was subsequently installed. In 1863, a new two-and-a-half-story keeper's dwelling was provided, attached to the light tower to provide convenient access during foul weather. In 1874, a second-class fog signal with two 18-inch engines and a Daboll trumpet was installed. This signal was in operation for 553 hours during 1875.

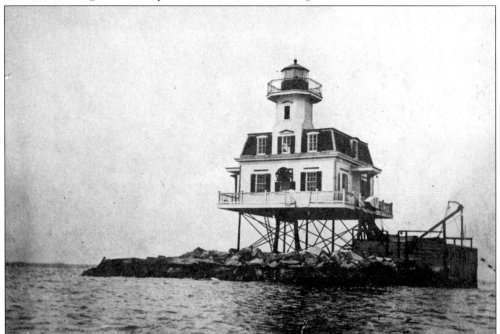

Long Beach Bar Light off Norwalk, was a beautiful screw pile–type family light station located at the entrance to Peconic Bay, at the eastern end of Long Island. The two-story dwelling consisted of a kitchen, dining room, sitting room, three bedrooms on the second floor, and an oil storage room. As was common at most lights, a cistern collected rainwater from the roofs for domestic use. The station was discontinued in 1948. Today only the iron piles remain.

Common sights along the coast include the various beacons, buoys, and daymarks provided to assist navigation in areas where a large lighthouse is not necessary. The Branford Reef Beacon was established in 1908 to mark the Branford Reef on the northerly side of Long Island Sound. Such beacons took various forms, many with a daymark on top and, in this case, a gas burning lens lantern to produce a fourth-order fixed white light.

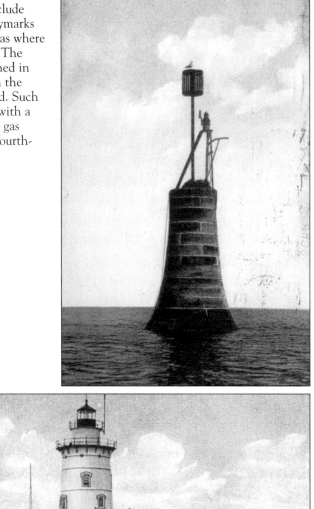

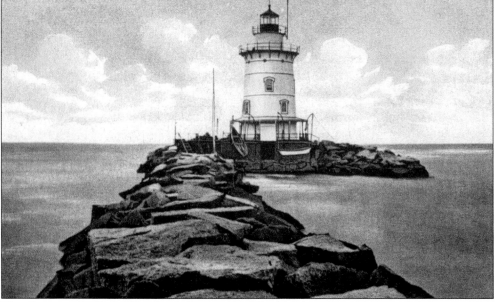

The Connecticut River has always been one of the largest and most important rivers in New England. It was navigable for vessels as far as Hartford, and considerable tonnage traveled via this route. Obstructing the mouth of the river is Saybrook Bar, a shifting bar of sand with water depths from two to nine feet. At the western side of the entrance, jetties were built to form a channel. The west jetty was marked in 1886 with what became known as the Outer Light.

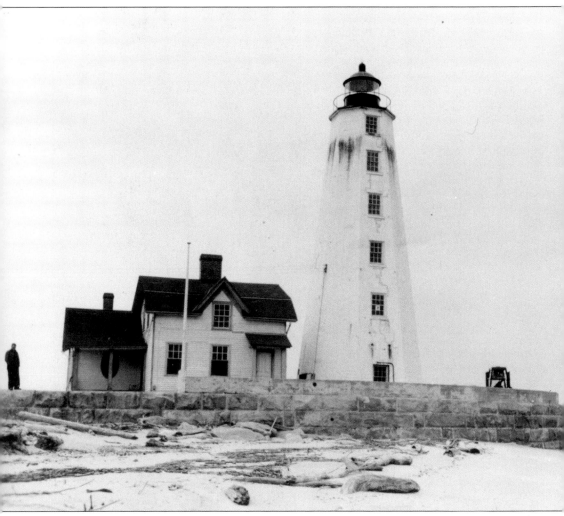

Near the inner end of the breakwater, the Saybrook Point (Lynde Point) Light was first constructed in 1803. The first lighthouse here was a wood structure that was 35 feet high, 20 feet in diameter at the base, and topped by an iron lantern. The light, which was first lit in August 1803, burned whale oil in its bank of seven lamps. By 1832, a new lighthouse was needed, but funds were not appropriated until 1838. The new lighthouse, called by residents the Inner Light, was completed and first lit in 1838. The granite structure was 25 feet in diameter at the base and rose 71 feet above mean high water. The light, similar to that in New London, is characterized by its octagonal shape and six windows rising up the south face. Although electricity was introduced to the borough of Fenwick in 1915, the light was probably not electrified until the 1940s or later. (National Archives photograph, c. 1885.)

The Inner Light at Saybrook included an attached one-and-a-half-story, gambrel-roofed affair that was built in 1858 for the keeper and his family. One early keeper of the Lynde Point Light was Daniel Whittlesey. After his death, his widow maintained the light here for some time before being replaced. The keeper would later be required to maintain both Inner and Outer Lights as a cost-saving measure.

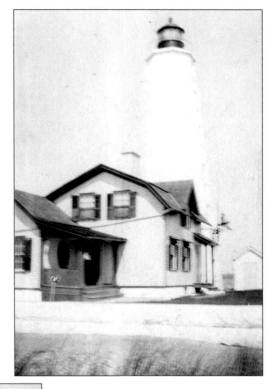

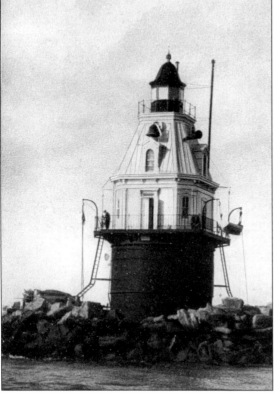

The Southwest Ledge, located in the middle of the main ship channel into New Haven Harbor, formed a great danger to navigation. To alleviate this, the U.S. Light-House Board constructed this beautiful structure in 1875–1877. The light, which represents one of the first uses of iron caisson construction, is of the Second Empire style, giving it the air of a domestic dwelling. It was surely one of the most beautiful lighthouses constructed at the time.

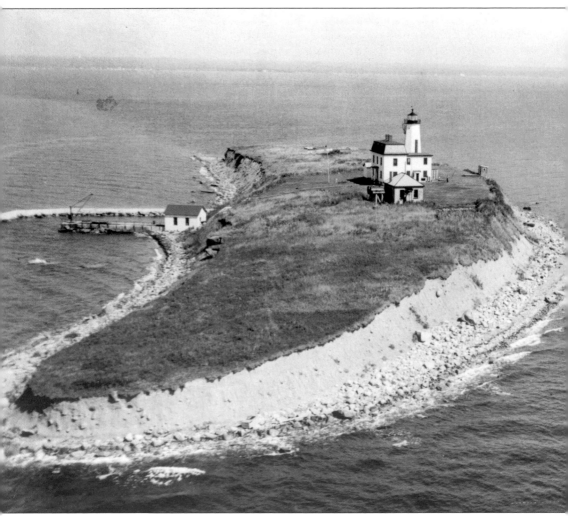

On November 6, 1851, Capt. Oliver Brooks was appointed keeper of the lighthouse at Falkner Island in Guilford. During his 31-year tenure, Brooks was credited with assisting more than 70 vessels in distress. In 1858, during a blinding storm, Brooks rowed to the rescue of four men aboard the wrecked schooner *Noah F. Webb*, for which he later received the Life Saving Benevolent Association's gold lifesaving medal. The first lighthouse on Falkner Island was erected in 1802, one of the first in the area constructed after the institution of federal control over Colonial lighthouses. At the same time, a six-room keeper's dwelling was constructed, which was replaced in 1871 with an eight-room, three-story dwelling. The tall octagonal light tower was topped by a 16-sided cast-iron lantern that was equipped with a fourth-order flashing white light. Falkner Island Light was noted as the site for many early fog signal experiments in 1865 and 1902. Joseph Henry, who was chairman of the U.S. Light-House Board at the time, used this site over the years to test various types of steam horns, sirens, whistles, and bells. (Courtesy Coast Guard Historian's Office.)

The 20-by-20-foot brick powerhouse, which still remains intact on the site, was provided with two steam-powered first-class fog signals after the 1902 tests and later with Dabol fog trumpets. In 1976, an electrical fire destroyed the 1871 keeper's house. Coast Guard personnel living there were subsequently moved to other quarters, but the tower and fog signal building remain today.

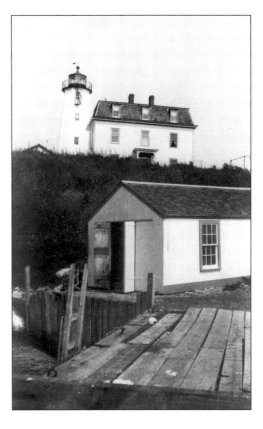

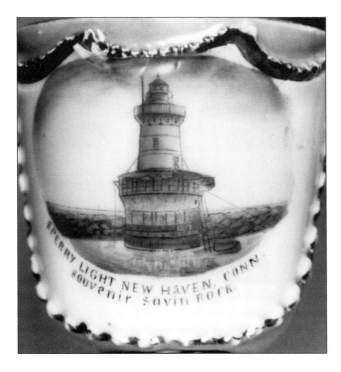

The New Haven Outer Breakwall, or Sperry Light, was built in 1899 to mark the westerly, or outer, breakwater at the entrance to New Haven Harbor. The breakwaters here have been the scene of a number of mishaps over the years. In 1906, during a severe snowstorm, the *C.H. French* came aground on the breakwater. The crews were forced to spend the night in the oil house to keep warm before aid could be summoned. This Sperry Light commemorative teacup dates from *c.* 1900. (Author's collection.)

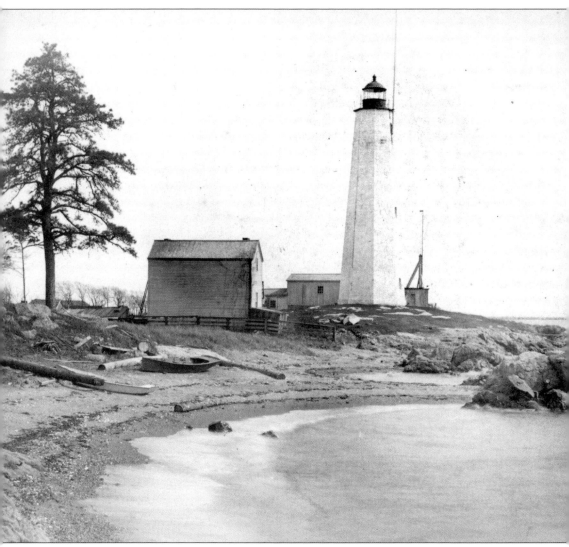

Of New Haven's four lighthouses, the one at Five Mile Point is the oldest, having been constructed in the early 1800s. The 1805 lighthouse stood at the extreme southeast corner of the harbor to mark the entrance and give direction around the Southwest Ledge. The tower was a wooden affair, octagonal in shape, and rose 30 feet to support eight oil lamps with 13-inch parabolic reflectors. By the 1830s, the lighthouse had become decayed and, in 1847, Congress appropriated $10,000 for a new 65-foot stone tower of East Haven sandstone with an attached keeper's dwelling. During the light's 77-year active career, there were many keepers stationed here, some for as short a time as three weeks. One keeper with a lengthy stay was Capt. Elizur Thompson. In 1860, Thompson was appointed keeper but, with the 1867 discovery of gold in Alaska, he left to try his luck. In two years, none the richer, he returned to spend the next 28 years in charge of the light. When Thompson passed away in 1897, his widow became keeper. After her death, her sister Adelaide Foster was appointed to replace her.

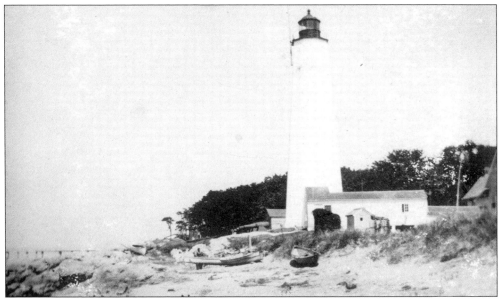

In 1877, the lighthouse on Five Mile Point was discontinued and was used for some time by the U.S. Weather Bureau to display storm warnings. Today the light still stands, painted white, and has become the focal point of the public park now in place. Efforts have been made to improve the beach for swimming, one of the few in the area, and this important and attractive tower may be preserved for generations to come.

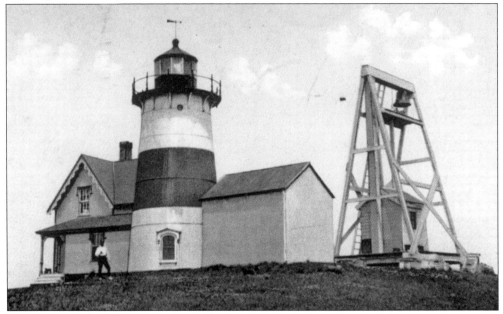

Five miles north of Middleground Light, on the west side of the entrance to the Housatonic River, lies Stratford Point Light. This area has long been dangerous due to the shifting shoals. The first light on this site was constructed by 1821. The wood-frame light tower was equipped with a fifth-order whale oil light. Later, a skeleton fog bell tower was added. In 1881, the tower was replaced by a modern cast-iron structure similar to those built on Tongue Point, Stamford, and Greens Ledge.

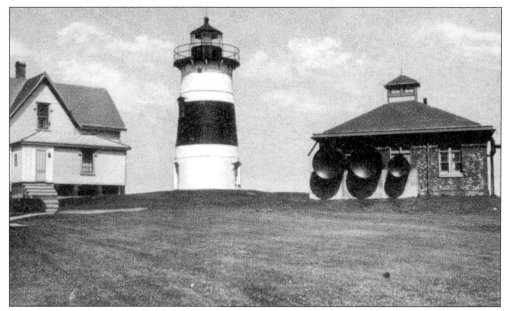

The light station here included the eight-room keeper's dwelling, the 1911 powerhouse, and the fog signal equipment. Early fog signals consisted of a large bronze bell, which would be struck by the keeper in times of fog. By the mid-1800s, mechanical striking apparatus was introduced, operated by a weight-driven clockwork mechanism. At one point, the Stratford Point keeper kept the fog bell operating for a full five days when fog and a blinding snow storm reduced visibility on Long Island Sound.

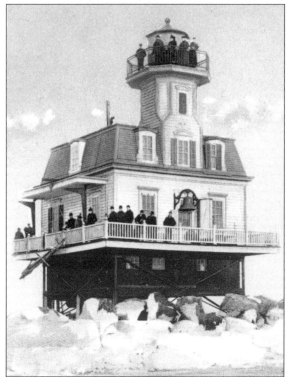

Bridgeport's first lighthouse was constructed in 1851 on the west side of the channel at the entrance to the harbor. The first light here was a wooden structure mounted atop iron piles, with an octagonal light tower rising from the roof. The structure was too small to house the keeper, which required him to row from shore each day when the weather permitted. It soon became apparent that a larger structure was needed and, by 1871, this new two-story dwelling was completed.

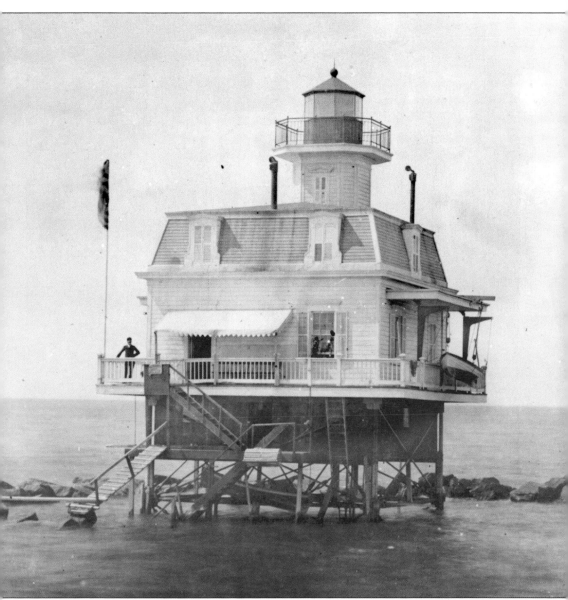

Rising from the roof of the dwelling was a fourth-order fixed red light, supplemented by a machine-driven fog bell when needed. For a time during the Spanish-American War, the government armed the lighthouse with a battery of guns to guard against attack by the Spanish. As late as the 1930s, the gun cradles still remained mounted on their cement cradles on the reef beside the light. As was common at Victorian light stations, weekend and summer visitors frequently traveled to lighthouses to view the wonderful sights and be refreshed by the coastal breezes. However, some years when the harbor froze over in the winter, visitors were also able to travel across the ice for a rare winter view from the light. (Courtesy Coast Guard Historian's Office.)

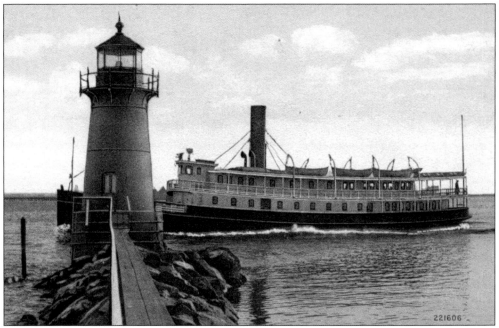

The Bridgeport Breakwater Light, or Tongue Point Light, was first constructed in 1891 on the tip of the old breakwater there. In 1919, the breakwater was demolished and the light moved to the eastern end of Tongue (Wells) Point. The conical iron tower, painted black, had a fixed white light that continues today. The light is one of the few remaining examples of this smaller 24-foot unlined cast-iron tower, which became a model for larger towers to follow.

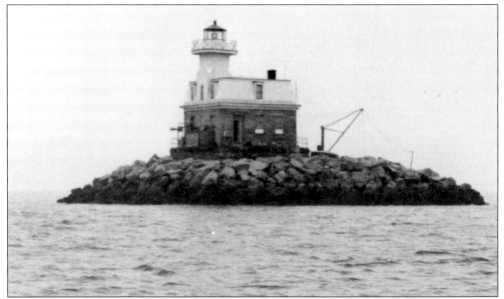

Another classic Victorian-style light was constructed in 1874 on Penfield Reef to mark the east end of the Fairfield Bar near the entrance to Black Rock Harbor. The elegant granite and wood structure rises 54 feet to its fourth-order lantern atop the roof. This was a family station. Twice during its history, the station listed the keeper's wife as the assistant keeper, a relatively rare occurrence in the U.S. Lighthouse Service. (Courtesy Coast Guard Historian's Office.)

The Greens Ledge Lighthouse was established in 1902 on the west end of Greens Ledge, making off from Sheffield Island in Long Island Sound. Numerous wrecks occurred here over the years until Congress approved the construction of a light in 1896. This light combined with that at Peck Ledge and five post lanterns to mark the channel entrance into Sheffield Harbor. Note the trumpet-shaped caisson that rises to form the gallery as two keepers pose for the camera.

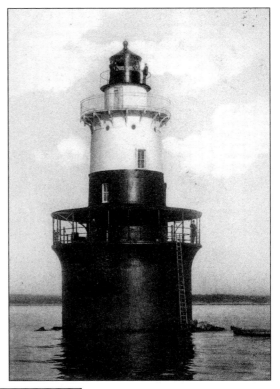

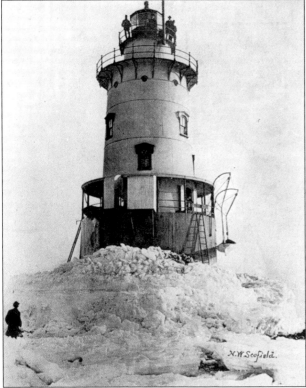

On the west side of the entrance to Stamford Harbor, a means was needed to mark Harbor (Chatham) Ledge for ships moving into the harbor. The U.S. Light-House Board determined that a lighthouse was necessary and, in 1881, construction was begun. The iron tower was fabricated at a Boston foundry and assembled on the site, atop a red concrete caisson. This typical "spark plug" light tower was painted white and was equipped with a fourth-order red fixed light.

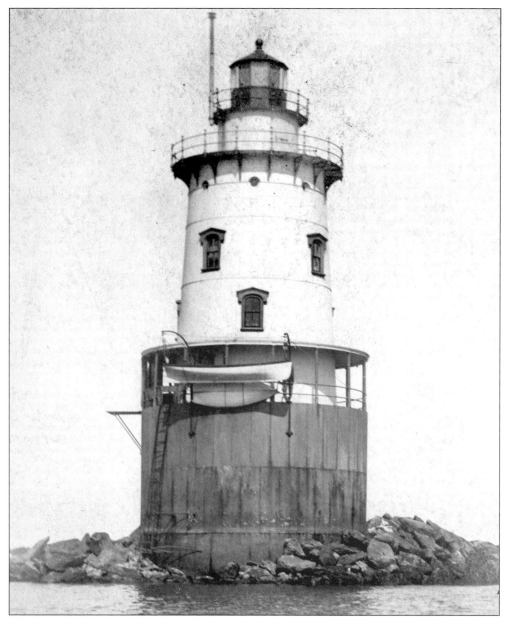

The Stamford Harbor Lighthouse became operational in 1882. Typical of this style light station, the cramped keeper's quarters, dampness, and isolation wore heavily on keepers. Over the next 25 years, 12 keepers were assigned to this location. In December 1929, an additional occupant came aboard the light. Despite the isolation and lack of medical care, Keeper Robert Fitten became a father here when his wife delivered a healthy son at the lighthouse. Note the station boat hanging from the davits in this c. 1880s view by H.S. Allen. When the lighthouse came under Coast Guard jurisdiction in 1938, Marty Sowle was retained as civilian keeper. In the fall of that year, Sowle sighted a boat in distress and made for the location in the station's 16-foot dory. He was able to rescue one of the occupants before he succumbed and soon delivered him to safety, for which he was awarded a Congressional silver lifesaving medal.

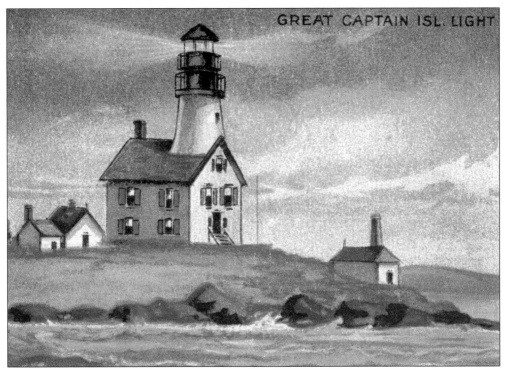

Great Captain Island sits just south of Greenwich, where Long Island Sound narrows to become the East River. Three major lights guard the area—New York's Execution Rocks Light, Stepping Stone Light, and Connecticut's Great Captain Island Light. This charming granite two-story light was built in 1868 and continued in use until 1970. Today the lighthouse is the home of the island caretakers. Shown here is a 1912 Great Captain Lighthouse cigarette card from a series of 50.

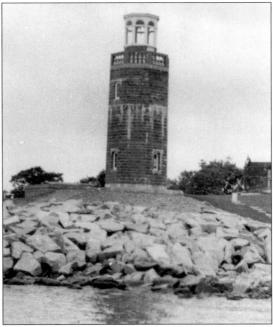

Avery Point lies in New London, once the location for the Coast Guard training station there. In 1943, this 55-foot ceremonial tower was constructed as a memorial to commemorate the Coast Guard's lighthouse history. From 1945 to 1967, it was lit as an aid to navigation. In 1960, the light was changed from fixed white to flashing green but was discontinued in 1967. Although the attractive stone light tower today sits unused and decaying, local restoration efforts have begun. (Courtesy Coast Guard Historian's Office.)

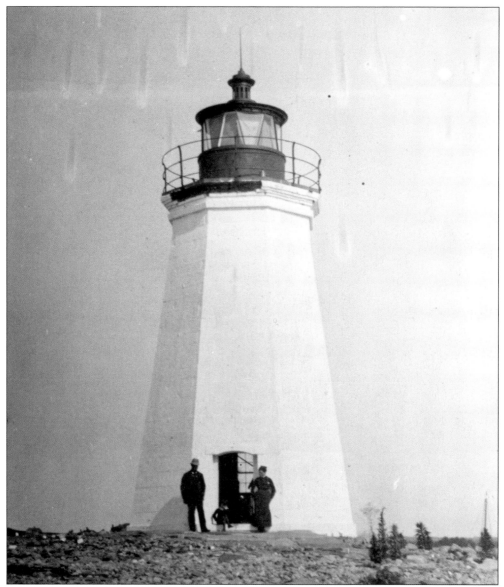

Not long after the federal government took over operation of the states' lighthouses in 1789, land was deeded for a light station on Fayerweather Island at the entrance to Black Rock Harbor in western Long Island Sound. Soon a wood-frame clapboard light tower was established on the south end of the island. The first light lasted 15 years until 1823, when it was rebuilt following a disastrous hurricane that "laid the lighthouse flat." Following the earlier destruction of the light tower, the present 40-foot octagonal tower was constructed on the same site. This new tower was constructed of sandstone blocks lined with laid-up rubblestone. When the light was electrified in the 20th century, a brick cornice with iron railing was added around the base of the lantern. Still visible today are the light tower and the foundations for the 1808 oil storage house and keeper's dwelling. Early lighting apparatus consisted of multiple lamps arranged on a circular iron rim, each with its own silvered parabolic reflector. The lamps utilized whale oil as their fuel, and later lard oil was substituted. (Courtesy Coast Guard Historian's Office.)

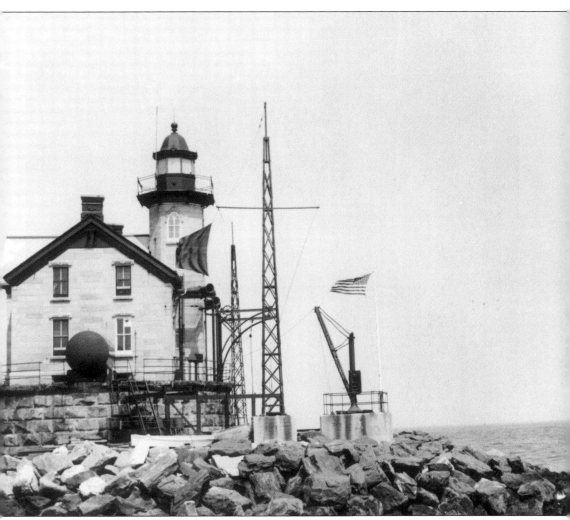

About five miles northeast of Old Field Point Lighthouse, in the middle of Long Island Sound, sits the Stratford Shoal, or Middleground Light. A light boat was first used to mark this gravel shoal in the 1830s and continued in use until 1877, when preparations were begun to construct a lighthouse here. The light is an elegant gray granite building. Its octagonal granite tower with a black fourth-order lantern rises from the southerly side of the dwelling. This design became a common one in exposed locations and provided a comfortable alternate for the keepers to the tall masonry tower living quarters. The exposed location of Middleground Light received the brunt of wind and seas driving up the sound and, combined with the many isolated winter months, wore heavily on the keepers stationed here. Note the storm warning flag flying from the mast and the hoist used to lift supplies aboard from the district tender. (Courtesy Coast Guard Historian's Office.)

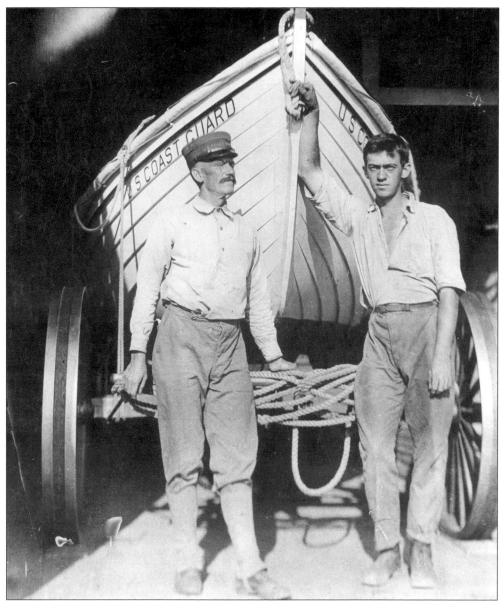

In this early-1920s photograph, two Coast Guardsmen take a break from their duties to pose in front of their surf boat. Boats used by the U.S. Life-Saving Service (and later the Coast Guard) were specially constructed for the purpose. They were made of cedar with white oak frames and were referred to as surf boats rather than the more common lifeboat. The boats had air chambers at each end for flotation and were fitted with cork fenders for protection during a collision with a wreck. The surf boat was pulled down the beach on its carriage by the crew, while some stations commandeered a horse for longer pulls through the soft sand. In the early years, lifesavers were fortunate when they were able to keep or borrow draft animals to aid them in pulling their apparatus through the sand, as the government rarely provided draft animals for the purpose. In some areas mules were used, but on Cape Cod horses were preferred. In later years, tractors were used for this task and, after World War II, Jeeps were used. (Courtesy Steve Marthouse collection.)

Eight

THE BIRTH OF THE
U.S. COAST GUARD

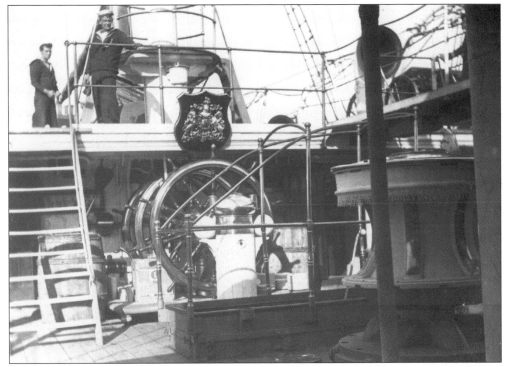

No book about the Life-Saving Service and early Coast Guard would be complete without a mention of their predecessor—the U.S. Revenue Cutter Service. In the 1780s, after American freedom had been won, the Continental navy was disbanded. A new sea force was therefore needed to enforce tariffs used to support the fledgling nation, to protect shipping from pirates, and to intercept contraband. On August 4, 1790, Congress established the U.S. Revenue Cutter Service. Pres. George Washington insisted on the appointment of only the most honorable men to command this new service, and the first such officers would come from the ranks of those who had served in the Continental navy. Secretary of the Treasury Alexander Hamilton created a fleet of 10 cutters and allotted $1,000 each for their construction. For two cutters expected to work in the New England area, an additional $500 was appropriated to construct them to be able to withstand the harsh New England storms and seas. By the end of 1791, 10 new revenue cutters were ready for service. For the next seven years, these revenue cutters formed the young republic's only armed force afloat. Shown in this *c.* 1890 photograph is the bridge of the Revenue Steamer *McLane*.

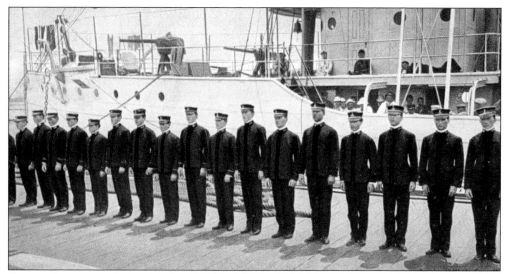

From its beginning, this new service performed a myriad of functions. By statute, the service was required to enforce almost every law bearing upon the maritime interests of the nation. Its duties embraced protecting customs revenue, searching for wrecked and missing vessels, suppressing mutinies, protecting property and fisheries in Alaska, protecting navigational aids along the coast, aiding the shipwrecked, patrolling the ice fields, and more.

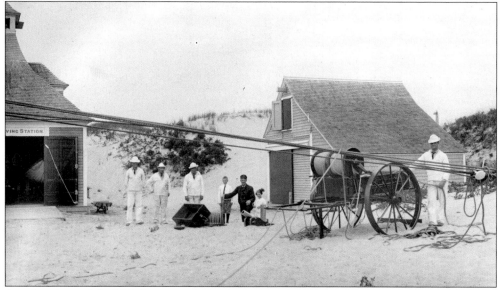

Another duty of the U.S. Revenue Cutter Service included the inspection and drilling of the lifesaving crews. Under the direction of general superintendent Sumner Increase Kimball, officers would periodically drill the lifesaving crews and investigate loss of life within the scope of the lifesaving operations. In addition, the Revenue Cutter Service worked to develop numerous lifesaving appliances that would become the mainstay of lifesaving rescue operations. (Courtesy Steve Marthouse collection.)

During wartime, the U.S. Revenue Cutter Service served as an adjunct to the U.S. Navy. Vessels of the service fought alongside the navy's vessels numerous times. During the Quasi-War with France, the Revenue Cutter *Pickering* captured 10 vessels in engagements with the French. Another cutter, the *Eagle*, captured five. During the War of 1812, a total of 14 British vessels were captured. Revenue cutters also made important contributions during the Seminole and Mexican Wars. (Courtesy John Koster collection.)

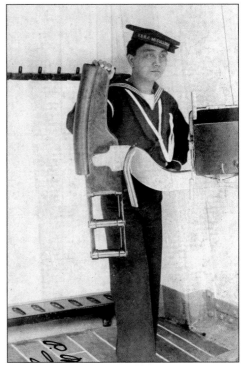

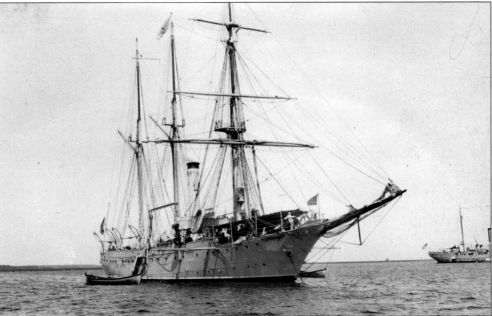

Following the Civil War, in which the Revenue Cutter Service saw an unprecedented expansion, Congress reorganized the service under a centralized administration. As booming coastal trade increased, with ever larger schooners wrecking along the coast, shipping interests began to demand improvements in the cutters, lifesaving services, and aids to navigation. Lifesaving services had begun to take shape as early as the 1790s in Massachusetts and, in the 1840s, along the shores of New Jersey and New York.

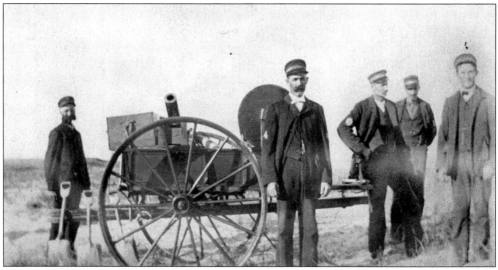

In 1871, the authority over both the U.S. Revenue Cutter Service and the fledgling U.S. Life-Saving Service was placed in a newly created U.S. Revenue Marine Bureau. Sumner Increase Kimball (then chief clerk) was selected to head the new bureau, where he would remain until 1876, when he became superintendent of the U.S. Life-Saving Service. One of Kimball's first actions was to inspect the existing stations. Most stations showed neglect and suffered from a lack of proper direction.

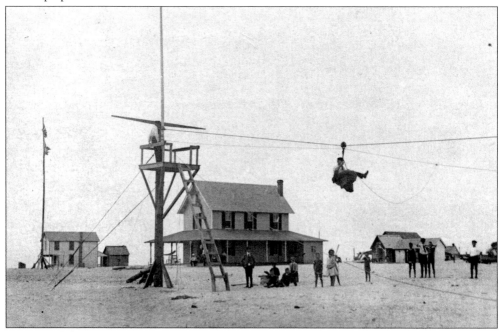

Convinced that the U.S. Life-Saving Service was capable of great good, Kimball set about the task of rebuilding the service. Soon Kimball had steered additional acts through Congress that were aimed at employing crews of experienced surfmen, building new stations, and purchasing new equipment. District Revenue Cutter Service officers periodically inspected the stations, drilled and tested the crews, and instituted lookouts and beach patrols. Next, Kimball would lobby Congress to authorize the establishment of a training school for new officers.

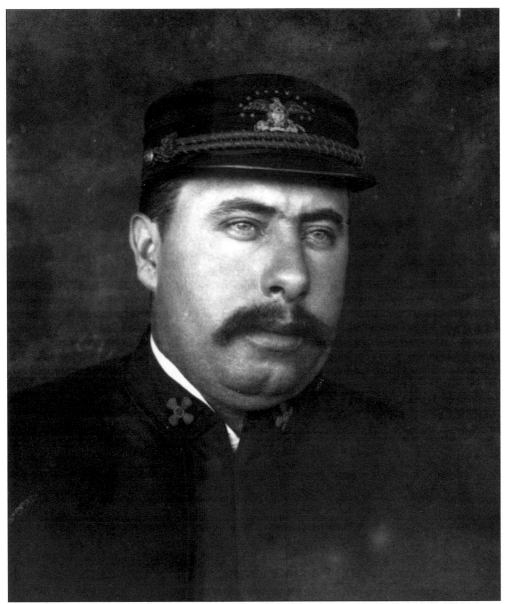

In the past, appointments to the officer corps of the U.S. Revenue Cutter Service had been made by the secretary of the Treasury, whose department was notoriously corrupt and riddled by political patronage. Although the federal government did not reform its hiring policies until 1883, the Revenue Cutter Service under Kimball had removed its incompetent personnel and revamped its hiring policies as early as 1871. But still more was needed. On July 31, 1876, Congress authorized a training school to ensure a steady supply of competent, well-trained officers. Today's Coast Guard Academy began as this Revenue Marine School of Instruction in 1876. Nine cadets began their training that year aboard the topsail Revenue Schooner *Dobbin*, which sailed out of Fisher Island. In May 1877, the *Dobbin* proceeded on a practice cruise with the first class of cadets. The *Dobbin* served as the school's training ship until late in 1878, when it was replaced by the 106-foot *Salmon P. Chase*. Shown c. 1890 is Lt. H.V. Butler, engineering officer aboard the Revenue Steamer *McLane*.

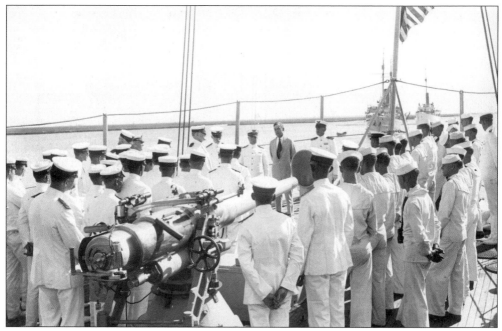

The course of study for cadets included daily academic courses, athletics, and practical experience. Courses included navigation, gunnery, small arms, seamanship, signalling, mathematics, law, history, and steam engineering. Cadets put to sea for a three-month cruise of instruction in which their endurance could be tested and much of their training could be put to use. On October 15, 1879, 6 cadets of an original 18 completed the two years of study and graduated.

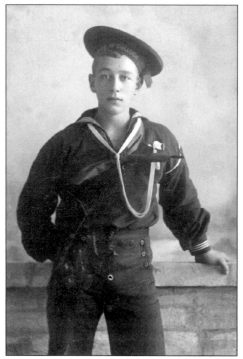

In 1878, Congress separated the Life-Saving Service from the Revenue Cutter Service and Sumner Increase Kimball was appointed general superintendent of the new lifesaving agency. Soon Kimball's efforts were to bear fruit; for within the scope of their operations in the first year, not a single life would be lost to shipwrecks. By the 1880s, the work of the lifesavers would reduce the casualties along the entire coast sixfold. Kimball would be long remembered for setting performance standards for years to come. Shown c. 1880 is a young Revenue Cutter Service seaman. (Courtesy John Koster collection.)

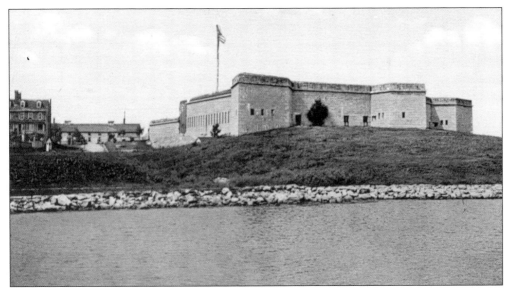

Late in 1900, Congress authorized money for land at Curtis Bay, Maryland, to create a permanent site for the School of Instruction. By 1910, however, the school would be moved to Fort Trumbull, an army coastal defense facility in New London, Connecticut. At this time too, after 30 years of service, the Revenue Cutter *Chase* was decommissioned and replaced by the *Itasca*, the well-known cutter that later communicated with aviatrix Amelia Earhart during her ill-fated flight.

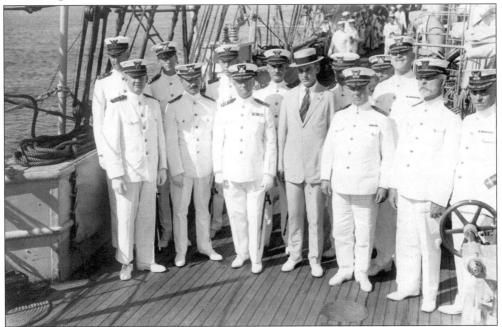

During the period from 1910 to 1915, Pres. William Howard Taft decided that the union of the Life-Saving Service and the Revenue Cutter Service would provide for the best protection of life and property at sea. In 1915, Pres. Woodrow Wilson signed into law the bill authorizing the union of the two services into the Coast Guard. In their last year of operation, the two services rescued 5,238 people, and the Coast Guard would continue their fine record to the present day.

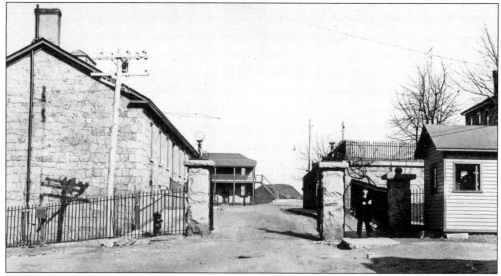

By 1922, the new Coast Guard Academy at Fort Trumbull needed to be moved once again to accommodate the increased size of the new service. However, it was not until 1929 that funds were appropriated to build the present facility at New London. By 1932, construction was complete and the academy began its operations. Despite changes over the years, two things have remained the same: cadets have always been selected on the basis of merit, and honor, professionalism, and excellence have always been emphasized.

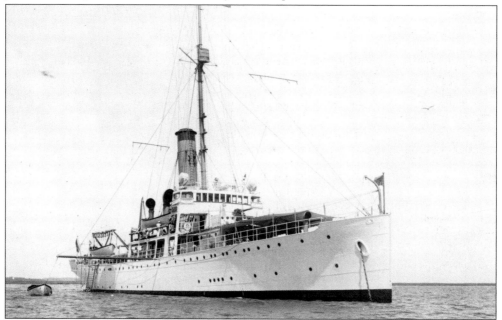

Through the 1930s, the existing lifesaving stations were operated by the Coast Guard in much the same manner as they had previously been run, continuing with beach patrols well into the 1940s. By 1938, the U.S. Lighthouse Service was abolished and its responsibilities were given to the Coast Guard. Although radio and other navigational improvements would lessen the need for such services over the years, even today shipwrecks occur along our shores to remind us of these earlier times.

Ida Lewis to the Rescue

The Mother is trimming her lamp above.
For the day is wild and drear;
That the Lime Rock Light may greet the night,
With its steady blaze of cheer.

The daughter sits at her work below—
For the girl is used to toil;
Plying her oar with a willing hand,
Or feeding the lamp with oil.

The mother looks on the angry sea,
And thrills to a sight of dread,
A sinking boat, with a drowning crew,
Mid billows that roll o'erhead.

But Ida, ready and prompt at need,
Has rescued many before;
Nor heeds the gale as o'er stone and weed
She flies to the rock-bound shore.

Her brow is bare to the beating rain;
She feels not the driving storm;
Though winds may moan and the gray gulls sail
And the wintry tide run strong.

Now quick to her boat, with practiced hand,
She launches the fragile bark;
It hath brought ere now through swelling seas
To the sinking man an ark!

Then Ida on! To the rescue spring!
Of the three! The boy is gone!
Though two still cling to the slippery keel,
Yet they cannot cling there long.

On, Ida! On! Though the billows rage!
For the prey so nearly won!
Yet your feeble arm shall cheat their wrath,
And your work of love be done.

The wreck is gained! The work is done!
Now back to the Light once more—
But thy deed to-day shall live for aye!
On many a distant shore.

—author unknown

Bibliography

Bachand, Robert G., *Northeast Lights, Lighthouses and Lightships Rhode Island to Cape May, New Jersey.* Norwalk, Conn.: Sea Sports Publications, 1989.

Brewerton, George D., *Ida Lewis, The Heroine of Lime Rock.* Newport, 1869.

Claflin, James. *Lighthouses and Life Saving along the Massachusetts Coast.* Charleston, S.C.: Arcadia Publishing, 1998.

———. *Lighthouses and Life Saving along the Maine and New Hampshire Coast.* Charleston, S.C.: Arcadia Publishing, 1999.

Dalton, John W. *Along the Coast.* Boston; Vol. 1. No. 1, March 1909; Vol. I, No. 9, June 1910.

Evans, Stephen H. *The United States Coast Guard 1790–1915.* Annapolis, Md.: U.S. Naval Institute, 1949.

Federal Writers' Project. *New England Hurricane, A Factual, Pictorial Record.* Boston: Hale, Cushman & Flint, 1938.

Flint, Willard. *Lightships and Lightship Stations of the U.S. Government.* Washington, D.C.: U.S. Coast Guard, 1989.

The Great Hurricane and Tidal Wave Rhode Island September 21, 1938. Providence: Providence Journal Company, 1938.

Hamilton, Harlan. *Lights and Legends: A Historical Guide to Lighthouses of Long Island Sound.* Stamford, Conn.: Wescott Cove Publishing, 1987.

Holland, Francis Ross Jr. *America's Lighthouses: Their Illustrated History Since 1716.* Brattleboro: the Stephen Greene Press, 1972.

King, Irving H. *The Coast Guard Expands 1865–1915.* Annapolis, Md.: U.S. Naval Institute Press, 1996.

Longo, Mildred Santille. *Picture Postcard Views of Rhode Island Lighthouses and Beacons.* Providence: Rhode Island Publications Society, 1990.

"Miss Ida Lewis, the Heroine of Newport." *Harper's Weekly.* July 31, 1869.

Munro, Wilfred H. *Picturesque Rhode Island.* Providence: J.A. & R.A. Reid, 1881.

"The New Lighthouse, New Haven Harbor." *Frank Leslie's Illustrated.* December 13, 1879.

Peterson, Douglas. *United States Lighthouse Service Tenders 1840–1939.* Annapolis, Md.: Eastwind Publishing, 2000.

Quinn, William P. *Shipwrecks along the Atlantic Coast.* Orleans: Parnassus Imprints, 1988.

Shanks, Ralph and Wick York. *The U.S. Life-Saving Service.* Petaluma, Calif.: Costano Books, 1996.

Snow, Edward Rowe. *Famous New England Lighthouses.* Boston: The Yankee Publishing Company, October 1945.

Thompson, Frederic L. *The Lightships of Cape Cod.* Northborough, Mass.: Kenrick A. Claflin & Son, 1996.

"The United States Life Saving Service." *Scientific American Supplement.* February 6, 1892.

"United States Lighthouse Establishment." *Scientific American.* June 11, 1892.

U.S. Coast Guard. *Annual Reports.* Washington: G.P.O., 1914–1926.

U.S. Life-Saving Service. *Annual Reports.* Washington: G.P.O., 1876–1914.

———. Mortar and Beach-Apparatus Drill. Washington: G.P.O., 1880.

———. *Regulations for the Government of the Life-Saving Service of the United States.* Washington: G.P.O., 1899.

U.S. Revenue Cutter Service. *Annual Reports.* Washington: G.P.O., 1800–1915.

U.S. Light-House Establishment [Service]. *Annual Reports.* Washington: G.P.O., 1846–1938.

For additional reading, the above original vintage titles and many others are available from Kenrick A. Claflin & Son Nautical Antiques, 30 Hudson Street, Northborough, Mass., 01532 (508-393-9814).

For additional information about these services, please contact the following organizations:

United States Life-Saving Service Heritage Association, P.O. Box 75, Caledonia, Michigan, 49316.

United States Lighthouse Society, 244 Kearny Street, San Francisco, California, 94108.

Shore Village Museum, 104 Limerock Street, Rockland, Maine, 04841 (207-594-0311).

The New England Lighthouse Foundation, P.O. Box 1690, Wells, Maine, 04090.